MOTHER'S HOUSE PAYMENT
- A MEMOIR

Content Copyright © 2012 Ronnie Schiller
Revised Ed. April, 2012

Special thanks to Paul Gilmartin and his
Mental Illness Happy Hour podcast
for helping me reach out with my story.
Blessings and love to you.

Introduction

"So, Ronnie, is it? That short for something?"

Suppressing the sigh that usually preceded my response to that oft-asked question, I smiled humorlessly. *No, it's not. That's why where it says "Full Name," I wrote "Ronnie."*

"No, it's long for 'Ron'," I offered. I was usually more polite aloud than in my mind. However, I supposed everybody was.

The man in the overstuffed chair in front of me awkwardly penned a note on the questionnaire I had completed in the waiting room. I was sizing him up, much as he was doing to me. I was cautiously optimistic. Of course, we had just met.

He was tall, lean, and much younger than I would have expected. I attributed his apparent youth to the fact that I was nearing my thirtieth year—everyone started to seem much too young as I progressed with my generation: rock stars, students, and even psychologists. I wistfully remembered that little Adam, whom I babysat for a dollar an hour when I was in junior high school, had recently graduated with a Bachelors degree.

The man who popped his head into the waiting area and called me back to his office was rather handsome. His smile was genuine and quirky, with a slight diastema in his front teeth. Slight gap, I noted, which is to say that it was not quite Lauren Hutton-esque, and far from the average cartoon hick.

His voice had a soothing, melted caramel quality. It resonated evenly like a gently plucked upright bass.

The most unexpected thing about the new psychologist was his skin. With the name Carlos Santo, I was expecting yet another Phoenix-area Hispanic gentleman. The man in the easy chair, balancing an open folder—my chart—on his knee, was a man of African-American descent.

I relaxed into the couch, skimming the supple, black leather-clad surface of the cushion beside me idly. I always had to touch everything. It drove my husband mad.

"Okay, Ronnie," Dr. Santo flashed that smile of his, "why are you here? What do you want me to do for you? What should we accomplish? "

I stammered for a moment, seeking the most concise response. No one had ever asked me what I wanted to accomplish; three psychiatrists and countless counselors and doctors had always applied their own agenda to "fix" me.

I made the appointment for a reason, and I told him so. I had reached a solid brick wall in my development, and I wanted over it. My life had weathered the emotional storm of the century throughout the past few years. The skies had cleared, but I wanted some direction. I knew my self-esteem problem was limiting me, and I knew that I couldn't work through it alone. If I trusted my own judgment in the least, I would have long since ended it all. The friendly little voice inside my head was no friend of mine. My personal relationships provided no respite from criticism.

I explained all of this to Dr. Santo, who took notes and occasionally scowled or nodded. He was reviewing my intake form while I spoke. It read like a much-clichéd plotline of a made-for-television movie of the week. My childhood was a horror story that I did not want to rehash with the guy. I didn't have enough life left to start from the beginning. I knew why I was all fucked up; I did not know how to change it.

"It looks like you've dealt with more than your share of pain," he remarked.

Oh, here we go.

I started to protest, but he lifted his gaze and continued to talk. He sounded as though he was going to deliver the grand plan.

"But that's not who you are. It's not even who you were. That's people you've known, experiences you've had, and learned responses to both," he shrugged dismissively, shaking his head. "Anybody who lives through the things you have will develop responses and reflexes. That's not why we're here."

"I'm listening." I was.

He handed me a pad of paper and a pen. I laughed at the logo from the drug company rep that had left it in the office. It reminded me of the branded pens my father always had in the pockets of his lab coat. That sort of marketing trinket can always be found in a doctor's office or hospital desk.

He told me to write on that paper a list of statements that defined me. Who I was at that time, not who I want to be, and not what someone else wanted me to be. He asked for at least seven things.

I was well into the study of who I was by the time I drove to his office. I began to write immediately. I soon had an honest list, all neatly contained with the yellow border that flowed from the copyrighted name of a drug that I recognized as a treatment for anxiety. I reached out to hand the paper to him, but he refused. He told me to read the list aloud. Suddenly, I was somewhat less sure of my choices.

"Ok, um," I stalled, "I'm a creative writer, a teacher, I am spiritual, I care about people, I am stronger than people think…"

"Whoa. That sounds kind of negative," he wrinkled his brow in disapproval. "Explain."

"I am strong. I am," I asserted, "but people usually don't think that when they meet me. I'm shy."

"Ok, I'll accept that one under protest. Go on."

"Strong, um...I am intelligent and love to learn. I am tolerant and accepting of people's differences."

"That it?"

"It's seven." I was going for minimum effort, and minimum bullshit.

"Good," he finished his notes and closed the chart. "I want you to put that list in your wallet or purse and read it every day. I also want to see you every two weeks, for now. Let's go make you an appointment, and you are free to go."

I folded the note and tucked into my wallet, certain that I would never look at it again.

As I drove home, my head was full of ghosts that had been awakened by the intake questions. I could almost pinpoint the moment when I lost my self-esteem: when I realized how awful I was. I'd answered the questions on the form about the times I had been hospitalized, and why. I listed the reasons for the medications that I was taking, the ones I had taken in the past, and the doses. I detailed all of the stressors in life, in order of severity.

My top stressor was waiting for me at home.

CHAPTER ONE: WHEN I REALIZED I NEEDED TO SWIM BECAUSE I WAS SINKING

I lived with a man who was contrary in every sense of the word. He was an obese, lazy, directionless co-dependent. He was my husband, and had held that title for three years. We had been living together for about twice as long as that.

Jason and I met while I was married to my high school sweetheart and he was married to the girl he impregnated at a party two years earlier. We were 21 years old, and shared a general dissatisfaction with our lives. We both needed attention that we weren't getting elsewhere.

Seven years later, I looked back on that simple disenchantment longingly while I braced myself for another divorce. I was ready to leave. Though it would surely be no surprise to Jason, I had not told him about my intentions. I didn't want to rock the boat too much, or risk another violent encounter. In addition to being familiar enough to dispense with common courtesy, he was twice my size and subscribed to the philosophy that the winner of the argument is the one who could most escalate the confrontation. Until I was able to escape to a safe distance, I just bit my tongue whenever he provoked me. I was biding my time.

I didn't have much tongue or time left.

As my birthday drew near, I spent a great deal of time in evaluative reflection. My managers and coworkers were impressed with my abilities, and always respected and supported my ideas. The contrast between the manner in which my new friends treated me, and the way my own husband treated me, became glaring. I realized that I was using work as an escape from home; similar to the way I used school when I was a teen. When I considered the facts from outside the context—from an outsider's point of view—my home life seemed twisted and wrong.

The fundamental truths of my relationship should have been more obvious to me. If one of my friends told me that they were being treated as I had been, I would rush to his or her defense. My instinct would drive me to protect my friend. The understanding that I had not even tried to do that for myself made such a life unbearable.

Subtle cruelties that previously evaded my attention became benchmarks, fortifying my decision to leave. An off-hand remark that seemed second nature to Jason would burn me all day. He would deliver little passive-aggressive jabs as I climbed into the car for the morning commute. Looking me over from the driver's seat, he would condescend.

"Don't you think you are a little big to be wearing that skirt?" He would not wait for my reply, which was to drop my head and slump in my seat in defeat.

Everyone at work complimented that skirt.

Jason's work history was ludicrously unstable. He was working at a convenience store when we met, but quit shortly after we moved in together. In the ensuing years, he had held numerous jobs in different industries, having been fired or quit for reasons only known to him. I proved my good character and acceptance of him as a person by not nagging or probing him about his work. The first year we lived together, he attached 10 different W-2 forms and an unemployment claim to his tax return. That was his response to being treated like an adult with free will.

In early April, he mentioned to me that he was thinking about quitting his job in the mailroom of a rebate-processing center. I knew this would be a mistake for him, as I would soon be unavailable to provide him with the financial support to which he had grown accustomed. I told him to talk to me before making any sort of decision on the matter, and he agreed. I thought we understood each other.

I was excused from work to celebrate my birthday, which fell on a Friday. A friend from the office was going to join me at a local amusement center for all the air-hockey, miniature golf, and go-kart racing that we could stomach. I asked Jason if he wanted to do anything that weekend. He was not interested, so I made plans on my own. I didn't really want to be around him, anyway. I was happy to sleep in, and meet my friend in the early afternoon. I bid Jason a good day as he left for work, and then curled into a ball under the covers.

I wasn't sure how much time had passed when I felt the weight in bed next to me, but it was still early. I sat up and looked with incredulity upon the still-clothed lump of Jason lying next to me. I was furious, but I knew that he had done it to himself.

"What—?" I spat.

Remaining motionless, he replied, "They were going to fire me, anyway, so I just quit. I think all the dust was bothering my asthma." His voice grew raspy, for effect as he added, "We'll be fine."

My decision was made. That morning, I realized that my life was being slowly dragged to the bottom by a selfish human anchor. I could not foresee any way to improve my life or become the person that I thought I could be with him tearing away at me. By Monday afternoon, I had located an apartment for myself in a quiet neighborhood on the west side. The rent was low, no credit check was required, and the area was safe.

I have always believed that the actions that are the easiest for us to take are the correct ones. Fate has a way of letting us know when we have screwed up by turning everything into an uphill battle. For me, telling my husband that I was leaving was refreshingly simple. I felt completely disconnected from the moment. As he drove us home, I laid it all out.

"I found an apartment today." I didn't even bother to cushion the blow.

"Oh, so how do we get out of our lease?" He wanted to make it harder. I know he did. Maybe he was hopeful, somewhere in a delusion.

"No," I corrected, staring out the windshield. "Not for us. For me: I'm moving out. I want a divorce."

The rest of the conversation was matter-of-fact. I wouldn't be moving into the new apartment for almost three weeks, so I would have time to pack, and to divide the property fairly. I didn't want to argue and fight. I wanted us to part amicably because I didn't hate him, nor did I love him—but I had, at one time. I was growing spiritually, and I had outgrown him. He seemed to accept my explanation, for the moment.

We began discussing the particulars of which appliance would belong to whom. Seven years of cohabitation had created an entanglement of debt and possession similar to the growth of scar tissue around a foreign body. There were sacrifices made, and most of them were on my side. I didn't care about possessions; I just wanted my freedom. I only wanted to ensure my survival.

"Let's just get this on paper, and be fair," I concluded, "Unlike last time."

I was referring to an incident that had taken place over a year prior, when he decided to leave me and explore his true self by living with his buddies and drinking constantly. It was one of the most painful experiences of my life because Jason had a clumsy, dishonest manner about everything he'd done in his life. Leaving me was no exception.

If you ask him today, he will tell you that I was at fault—of course, he lies. In a proximal way, I suppose I started it. In the playground moral structure of six-year-old children, he would have been justified in what he did to me. We were adults, but he still reasoned like a kid trying to get out of detention for causing a bloody nose. He managed to avoid taking responsibility for anything in his life.

One of the markedly frightening aspects of bipolar disorder is the fact that the moods feel so real. You know, because you feel; you believe because you know. Doctors always warn against stopping the medication because this is the common reaction to hitting a delicious stretch of mania. The sufferer feels so good. You are everyone's favorite person, the life of every party, the center of attention. You are brilliant and productive, brazen and clever. You are unstoppable, and invincible. You are just shy of God and making your way to dispose of Him. You feel that good.

When you are running at top speed, nothing annoys you more than a wet-blanket naysayer. The slow, stupid, resistant-to-change people become gadflies at your picnic. They must be cast aside in the name of perpetual motion. This is not an act committed out of cruelty; it is a necessity. You can't be expected to stop and judge or plan. There are no consequences for the person who moves on before the fallout hits.

I have oft compared extreme mania to the feeling one would get from being in the control seat nestled in the head of a giant robot. The controls do not respond, and you can only watch the view screen helplessly as your creation destroys your life.

I was in this very situation in the fall of 2000, riding a mania precipitated by the use of over-the-counter diet energy pills. I was struggling with my weight, and an early success with the diet pills led to regular use. Unfortunately, the stimulants opened the door for mania, which crept in quietly and staked a claim with little or no protest from my medication. The sad fact is that the chemistry project that is my brain had been running unchecked for years. By the time the dieting began, I was well on my way to a seasonal swing.

I had transformed into the life of the party, and my social life began to expand. Since Jason was the wet blanket in my liquor-fueled lust fests, he was not invited when I went out drinking and carousing each weekend. I was partying like a single woman, though not in a sexual sense. I was selfish and considered no one when I made plans or accepted invitations.

During that time, I required little or no sleep. I attended college full time, worked a full-time day job, and began a part-time night job as a phone-sex operator. I worked out of my home in the employ of an out-of-state company. I spent six-hour shifts, logged in to their phone system from my office with a headset on. While I was chained to the phone, I would write papers and carry on Internet chat conversations to fill the time between calls.

I was chatting when I met Todd. He was a few years my junior, and interested in the one thing mothers warn their daughters to avoid. He made no qualms about this. I had never learned to differentiate between sex and affection, so I thought he was romantic.

Meanwhile, my party buddies hated Jason because he was the authoritative figure. I was the fun-fun party girl, and he was seen as the frumpy disciplinarian. No one ever had anything good to say about Jason in my presence, and I agreed without question. The attitude that I would be better off without him was cultivated healthily in all of that fertilizer.

Todd and I exchanged cell phone calls carelessly—mainly concerning when I would be able to meet him so he could close the deal. I was stalling the encounter—not because I felt a moral obligation, but because he lived too far away. He sometimes masturbated while we spoke to each other. It made me feel naughty and desirable. In hindsight, though, I'm sure he did that to anyone who would talk to him.

One evening I ended up with the usual crowd at an upscale club on the east side, jammed into a booth with six other people. The place was packed with Scottsdale's typical elite and beautiful: white people of privilege. Feeling very out-of-place, I was slinging back eight-dollar shots of Patron Silver as fast as the smarmy waiter could bring them.

I tried to appear comfortable, chatting with the company hottie to my left. He worked in Human Resources and resembled a bulky Clark Kent. We had to lean over and speak into each other's ears to converse over the club noise. It's amazing how liquor can dissolve your personal space, along with your common sense and good judgment.

Before I knew what was happening, he had leaned over and inserted his tongue into my ear. I chalked it up to a prank, and laughed it off. He continued to do it throughout the night, but there was never a context to it. I thought he was trying to be funny, and I wanted to be too cool to react. I had done silly things, myself, when intoxicated.

At the end of the evening, I had to drive him home. He was too drunk to drive his expensive car home to his parents' half-million dollar condominium. I wasn't much better off, but I was too manic to believe in consequences. On the drive to his place, he proceeded to tell me how he'd been watching me at work, and what specific outfits of mine were his favorites. I was deeply confused by every word he said.

"Did you ever think that the day would come that you would be coming to my house to have sex with me?" He said this without the slightest humor, and then reached over and stroked my right breast. I remember gripping the steering wheel as if it were a life preserver.

My eyes were the size of saucers when I looked in the rear view mirror to check on my girlfriend who was driving my car behind us.

I pulled her aside in the driveway and told her not to leave us alone. I didn't want to fish off the company pier, but I know I would have made use of his pole, if left alone. She agreed to protect me, laughingly. We got the grand tour of his parents' very nice home. He was subtly angling for a three-way, the whole time. My friend and I politely made our escape after some quick small talk.

As we walked out of the garage, he pulled me back in, and pinned me against the wall. He kissed me on the mouth and neck, and wrapped his hand around mine so he could press my palm against his very large erection. I was surprised, aroused, and scared altogether.

When my girlfriend honked my car's horn, I left him to fend for himself without a word. I spent the rest of the weekend in a daze, and my courage catapulted beyond reason. Clark Kent was a gateway drug.

A week later, I went out for drinks with the same girl and arranged for her to drop me off at Todd's place for the night. I drank enough to convince myself that I really wanted to take that leap with Todd.

I was full of booze and bravery when I met him in the driveway. We had to sneak in quietly, so as not to disturb his roommates. He was drunk, too. Sex was messy and rushed. I was wearing a bra with crossing satin cord in the front and he nearly succeeded in breaking it apart because he couldn't figure out how to get the thing off me. I don't think I ever touched his bed. The whole experience was demeaning to the point of nearing rock bottom.

In the middle of the festivities, my cell phone began to ring. I had to crawl across the floor to silence it, and I noticed that it was Jason calling. Todd was undeterred by the distraction. Soon, Todd was sprawled over the bed, snoring. I was on the floor, hugging my knees in the dark and freezing. I waited for morning to come so I could go back to my girlfriend's place.

The ride in Todd's Bronco back to my car was depressing. It wasn't worth the cheating for such a lousy lay: I had no positive feeling to comfort me. In the morning light, he was unappealing with greasy hair, rotting teeth, and rough features. I wanted to throw myself onto the freeway.

Jason suspected where I had been, and I knew I had gone too far. When I returned to the car, I found sun-wilted roses and a sappy card in the driver's seat. I couldn't accept the shame of his loving gesture. I scarcely felt that I deserved to draw air, much less to accept love. I dropped both on the ground outside the door and drove away.

I had reached the point of no return, and then sprinted well past it. I felt I had no choice but to leave, and set out to do so. My girlfriend and I searched for a place where I could live near the apartment she shared with her boyfriend. I had a crush on him, too. I was short-circuited by experience so that I felt physical attraction to people of whom I was fond. I didn't know how to be friends. If I'd had the chance, I would have ruined that friendship.

I made plans to move, and went through the motions of planning transportation to work. My deepest intention was to move away, so I could be alone—and finally, I could kill myself in privacy. No one could intervene. I had little interest in living alone.

Jason suffered terribly through all of these exploits. He was in the living room, looking half-starved, weeping, and begging me to stay when I returned home from an interview with a potential roommate. I was tired of running, and generally worn out. When he asked me to stay and told me all would be forgiven, I was actually relieved. I gave in.

Depression follows mania. A manic person falls like Icarus, plummeting away from the sun into the depths of the sea. Deeply, darkly, completely the sufferer is consumed until nothing of that sense of godliness remains. A hollow, hopeless, terrified suffocation prevails. There is no lifeline to cling to, and no motivation to grasp it, anyway. One is so low that the idea of living one more moment is overwhelming.

I was falling into what would be the most severe bout of depression in my life the first night that Jason did not come home from the bar near his work. He called shortly after eleven o'clock that night. I was panicked and upset because I had just discovered that he had unleashed a virus on our computer. He had been duped into opening an email with a supposed pornographic attachment, and infected the system that I needed in order to transmit my homework. I was angry, and worried. I had never dealt with a virus before. I barked at him on the phone, and he hung up on me. When I called him back, he assured me that he would be home shortly; he was having a beer with his buddy.

After waiting up for several hours in tearful agony, I called his voicemail. When he failed to respond, I called several times, weeping and begging him to call me back. I received no response to the multitudes of voice messages I left on Jason's cell phone, so I began to call everyone else I knew. It was a short list. I had severed contact with my friends at Jason's insistence. I wanted to find someone to tell me that everything was going to be all right.

I called a mutual friend of ours named Floyd, but was destroyed by his sharp response.

"He is probably leaving you, and it's probably because of something you did!" He growled his verdict with disgust before hanging up on me.

Floyd was an alumnus of the same college Jason had attended with my encouragement (and on my dollar) before we left Utah. We were close, and became more so when Floyd moved to Phoenix and shared our apartment for a few months. Even though he was nearly my father's age, I felt equal to him and spiritually tethered to him as though my life depended on it. I believed that Jason envied our connection, and that was the reason we vacated the apartment and left Floyd behind to live in his car. It hurt, but didn't dare to challenge Jason. The painful tone of disgust and anger in Floyd's accusation hurt me to my soul.

I was exhausted and paralyzed with fear in my depressive state. My husband didn't come home in the morning. This became his habit for several weeks. He would come home briefly around six in the morning, and ignore my pleas for him to talk to me. Worse, he would come in reeking of alcohol and want to have sex—to which I would comply, vainly giving everything I could to keep him. The cloying smell of beer and liqueur shots turned my stomach, and I wept quietly while he was on top of me. I offered him the only thing of value I thought I had, no matter how it bruised my spirit. However, he never stayed.

One early Sunday afternoon, he told me he was running to work to pick up some papers. I begged him not to go, or to take me with him. He laughed at me, and promised he would be back.

After a couple of hours, I called him and he said he was on his way. He never showed.

This behavior continued for weeks. I stopped eating because the constant anxiety and distress made it impossible to keep food down. I couldn't sleep, and spent hours in bed, watching the clock and listening for any sounds outside that might indicate his return. I had pains in my chest, and trembled all over. I missed work because I wanted to be in the house, should he return. I didn't want to be alone. I began to show physical symptoms of lithium toxicity: headaches, tremors, and diarrhea. I could taste metal in my mouth.

I spoke to a friend of his on the phone, and learned that Jason had been spending the night with one of the girls from his class. I was furious, but I would have agreed to forgive and forget, as he had promised to do for me.

I left my job and drove across the valley to his workplace to show him how reasonable I was about the situation. That is the logic of mental illness. I was desperately clawing at the retreating threads of my sanity, and trying to win back a husband I should never have wanted in the first place by demonstrating how reasonable and accepting I was. I drove for 45 minutes, shaking, crying, and talking to myself frantically in order to show him how well I accepted his affair with this young girl.

When I confronted him at work, he sent me away angrily. He assured me that his relationship with this girl was only platonic. I wanted to speak to her, thinking she would see what a good person I was and lose interest in my husband. He refused, and promised to talk to me about it at home. He didn't come home that night.

In the lean hours of the morning, the anxiety led me to call the local crisis line. I just needed someone to talk to, to help me calm down so I could make it through the night. They said they couldn't help me unless I was planning to kill myself right away. I curled into a ball and cried for hours.

The next morning, Jason came in with that bar stench hanging around him. He wanted to watch pornography, and wanted to have sex with me. I obliged him without question. He was rough and hateful, insisting on forceful anal sex because he knew I wouldn't say no. I felt that I deserved it. He told me he wanted to arrange a threesome, and bring another girl in so he would have something good to look at, at least. I said that would be fine, though it devastated me to hear it.

We rose from bed and followed the usual custom, walking to the bathroom and the vanity. When I asked him what I could do to get him to come back home, he cruelly suggested that I have his baby. Cruel, because I had my fallopian tubes removed in the middle of my mania the year before. He might as well have asked me to jump out the window and fly.

Somehow, I persuaded him back to bed to spend the day there with me, using me as he wished; so long as he stayed. He had just agreed when the phone rang. His grandmother had suffered a stroke, and she wasn't expected to live much longer. He was advised to visit her as soon as possible. He said he'd make the ten-hour drive that day.

I convinced him to take me along, saying that his grandmother loved me and I had a right to see her as much as he did. This was true. I also wanted to see my parents—my father and his wife, Sara, who lived near there. Sara and I were always very close. I called her "Mom." I had been calling them every night while I waited for him, hoping they could keep me grounded. I wanted to see Mom, as a little child does. Therefore, this was also true. The real reason for going was being able to spend ten hours with him—more than I had seen him in three weeks.

I got an advance on my paycheck from work to pay for the trip, and the car needed new tires, so I took care of that. He had to go to work to straighten things out before he left. I sat at the tire shop in imminent danger of vomiting water and pure acid, horrified that he would leave without me. I should have been so lucky.

Before we even left town, he told me that the girl he'd spent the night with, Missy, was off-limits for my comments. He'd brought along a huge CD collection that he'd borrowed from her—all Dave Matthews, Sara McLachlan, and Macy Gray— a big difference from the stuff he usually liked. Typical affair behavior. He told me that he'd discussed the relationship with her. They had feelings for each other, but they couldn't act on them because he was married to me. I began to sob, because I knew that I wouldn't be a problem for long, the way things were going.

He told me that he would push me out of the car and leave me there if I kept crying. I stopped, holding my breath, not because I was afraid to be pushed out of the car. I already felt as if he had done that. I was afraid of being left behind.

The trek from Phoenix, Arizona to Ogden, Utah took us through Las Vegas. Jason's childhood buddies, a husband and wife, lived there. As we approached the valley, Jason urged me to smoke a joint and calm down so I could put a happy face on for his friends. Surely, after all those years, we couldn't let on that he was behaving badly. He wasn't accounting for the fact that marijuana is a depressant.

Soon, I was back to sobbing, though quietly. I felt entirely removed from my body, as if my soul had long since given up on me. We were listening to Sarah McLachlan sing about her husband. Every word was like a sting. It was like riding through darkness, locked in the center of his affair.

The visit to his friends' place went over pretty well, though I knew the wife suspected something. She was a big, brash, rough kind of girl, but she seemed to be attuned to my feelings. I don't think I've ever felt as close to her as I did on that visit. In the morning, before we left Las Vegas, Jason called Missy to have a long, private conversation with her on his mobile phone. When I tried to approach him as he paced on the sidewalk with the phone pressed to his ear, I was ordered away.

The rest of the trip was like a walking nightmare for me. I had to keep quiet about what was going on between us, and behave as normally as possible. I still couldn't eat, and was prone to bursting into tears. The greatest humiliation came when we visited his aunt and uncle. I should have known better, and I will never live down the spectacle I created.

I was keeping mostly silent while he chatted with his favorite aunt, a cool older chick with animal-print furniture and fake zebra rugs, and her reformed biker husband. We all sat at the kitchen table, passing around a marijuana pipe. Smoking more weed made me feel stretched like the taffy you see in the window of a candy shop, twisting and thinning. Jason got on the phone with another of his aunts, and took the phone out of the room, down into a stairwell, to talk to her in privacy.

When no one was looking, I crept over to watch Jason as he spoke on the phone. I had to keep him in sight. I heard him telling his aunt about Missy: how wonderful he thought she was, and how brave and brilliant. I almost fainted, collapsing into my chair. I was shaking so badly that my legs were convulsing. I couldn't see, and I just said, "Oh my God!"

By this point, they were both worried about me, having no idea what was wrong with me.

I said, "Jason is telling Aunt Teri about his girlfriend! I can't believe this. With me right here!"

Jason's uncle tried to reason with me, saying, "Jason doesn't have a girlfriend, he's married to you! And if he did, he wouldn't tell Aunt Teri about it."

I realized how ridiculous I must have looked to them. They didn't know. I stumbled toward the front door, apologizing. I was beyond embarrassed.

The only good thing about that whole trip was being able to sleep in a bed with someone next to me for a couple of nights. It was light sleep, for I feared that he would leave me there, but it was sleep.

Before we headed south to visit my parents, we went shopping. The advance from my check wasn't going very far, so I didn't buy anything for myself. I was disappointed, but practical. Jason bought several items for himself: clothes, CDs, a portable CD player. He also bought the sappily sickly romantic Dido CD for Missy, and hid it in the car until we were on our way home. Fucking Dido. Upon discovering it, I was angry that I had forsaken myself, and hurt. I began to cry again, and I was silenced by the same threat as before.

Mom was worried about me, and had little to say to Jason. She told me he was mistaken about his relationship with this young girl because he thought there was more to it than the girl really did. My stepmother knows things. Still, she gave me a sandwich bag with a handful of sleeping pills and antidepressants to help me get through. I wanted to stay with my parents, but I was compelled by the possibility of saving my marriage.

The closer we got to Phoenix, the more shaken I became. I knew once we returned home, he would leave me again. I made him pull over a couple of times, so I could dry heave on the side of the road. As we approached Phoenix, I told him that I was thinking about killing myself. I was. I said that maybe I should go into the hospital or something to get help. I couldn't handle the stress and depression, alone.

He told me if I did, he would leave for good. My stress grew.

We had not even unpacked our bags when I found him on the phone with Missy. Hearing the way he spoke to her punched me in the stomach: so intimate, and sweet. She had no idea what he was really like, and she probably never would. He was arranging to meet her, as I sat right in front of him. I had the impression that he was enjoying making me suffer, but I was too weak to defy him. He left, again, moments later. He didn't bother to lie about returning, and I didn't care to ask.

The night was too long, and full of noises and phantoms. If a bipolar sinks far enough into a mood, they begin to hear voices. I had only experienced the auditory phenomenon a couple of times in my life, and I think that night was one of them. It sounded to me as if I could hear someone in the living room, downstairs; perhaps the TV was on. I was too frightened to check on it, and lay tensed in a curled mass of adrenalin and anxiety. I cried constantly and talked to myself in an attempt to bring order to my chaotic, irrational state of mind. I told myself that I would be safe as long as I stayed on the bed.

The anxiety reached its apex in the hour between two o'clock and three o'clock in the morning. At that time, I knew the bar was closed, and I could almost convince myself that Jason would be coming home. I pled with God for the power to exert my will over him and make him come home. Every minute that passed after that was a minute closer to the sound of his key in the lock of the front door. On that night, it never came.

The sun rose as it always did, and shone through the window upon my battle-weary body lying stiff on the bed. I understood that he was working by that time, and would not be home. The silence of our townhouse nagged at me in the way that a constant noise can irritate the ears. My imagination was limited by the dark view of the depression that held me, leaving me without hope. I didn't want to live alone. I couldn't live alone. I despised the wreck that I had become, so weak and anxious that I couldn't work, eat, or leave the house. I just sat around talking to the walls, crying, and pulling at my filthy hair with trembling hands. It was no way to live.

I picked up the empty glass from the headboard shelf, and walked to the vanity. I refused to look myself in the eye as I filled the glass with stinking Arizona tap water. Returning to the bed, I used the water to swallow the contents of the sandwich bag my mother gave me, along with some of my medication for good measure. I knew it wasn't enough to kill me, but that was not my intention. I wasn't trying not to live; I was trying not to live alone.

I called the crisis line again, prepared with an affirmative response as to whether or not I was going to endanger myself. Like uttering the magic word, I received a response within minutes. A mixed gender team arrived with a county van to cart me away. I didn't ask where we were going as I followed them to the parking lot. I was overcome with relief and a sense of security.

We ended up in an emergency room in south central Phoenix, waiting for the doctors. I completed some paperwork for the lady van driver as we sat in awkward silence. I have never really learned what sort of small talk is appropriate under the circumstance that you have just tried to kill yourself. You'd think it was second nature.

When the doctor took over, the van people made a quiet retreat. The doctor seemed annoyed to have to deal with me. I felt it, and understood: he had to take care of patients who had been injured in accidents, and had little time or sympathy for self-inflicted issues. I knew his type, and I didn't care. People surrounded me again, and I didn't care how they felt about me or what they did to me because anything was better than being alone.

The lanky, balding, bespectacled doctor in charge of my emergency care ordered a phlebotomist to get some blood samples and vanished, having assessed the minor threat of overdose. Processing the samples would take hours, during which time I slept. I slept like Huckleberry

Finn dozing on a raft in the middle of the Mississippi River on a slow summer day. I never felt such release in slumber, before or since that day.

I wasn't certain of the hour when my caretaker woke me, but I sensed a decline in the amount of natural light in the common area. He informed me that my blood pressure was high, and that my blood lithium level was in the toxic range. I was fortunate, in that their mental health unit had a bed for me. An orderly was going to escort me to the lockdown wing, shortly. I dozed while I waited, and wondered if I would regret what I had done.

By the time we were crossing the skywalk that linked the main hospital with the mental hospital, I was having serious doubts about wanting to spend any time locked up. It tends to damage one's career, being in a lockdown for a week or two. Moreover, I still wanted to save my marriage.

He ushered me to the reception desk for the unit. The desk was a tall, wood-laminate structure with room for three. It was situated in the corner of an open lobby full of couches and over-stuffed armchairs and a television that I assumed was permanently tuned to the Lifetime network. Floor-to-ceiling windows overlooked a lush courtyard full of old trees with benches beneath them. The entrances to places like these were always designed to look idyllic so that the families felt better about having their loved ones locked up. The rotund woman behind the counter greeted me with learned courtesy, and left to fetch a counselor for me. When she returned, I decided to make my move for the door.

I asked her if I could leave of my own free will, since I brought myself in. She said I could, under the condition that someone came to pick me up. She pushed the telephone on the counter toward me, picked a line that was open, and plopped back into her chair. I called Jason's cell phone, hoping he would answer.

I could tell by the cheery "Hell-o!" that he had no idea who was calling. I tried to sound very calm and friendly to avoid offending him as I explained the situation: I was at the admitting desk of a mental hospital in south Phoenix because I was going to kill myself. They would let me go, if he would just pick me up. He broke in, full of venom.

"Do you know what time it is?"

I did not, and I told him so without bothering to point out that I had been unconscious in the emergency room for the past several hours.

"My shift starts in ten minutes. I am not jeopardizing my job to come get you. You did this to yourself, so you are on your own!" In closing, he added, "Fuck you! Don't call me again."

As I hung up the phone, I experienced true defeat and sincerely wished to die. As such, I submitted willingly to the intake process. I was awash in humbling aloneness.

When people imagine mental institutions, they usually conjure up the stark white rooms and barred windows of famous films; places full of pajama-clad lunatics, drooling and raving to themselves as they shuffle in a disconnected delirium. In reality, this is hardly the truth—even less so in private hospitals. The adult lockdown ward at St. Joseph's hospital was a bustling collective of emotionally crippled human beings, who were still human despite their myriad worries.

I arrived at the end of dinner, and the common area and patio were packed with my fellow patients and future roommates. I kept my gaze fixed on the table before me as I spoke to the counselor who was processing me in, but was aware that others were staring. I was new, and I probably looked like hell.

The check-in process reminded me of entering prison. He took an inventory of all of my possessions, which was quick, considering I had only my purse on me. I had to describe each item of value and determine whether it would be stored in the safe or if I would keep it with me. The cell phone and my wallet went into the safe; my wedding ring, and watch stayed with me. Also recorded was Jason's watch, which had been in my purse since the trip to Utah. I chose to keep that with me, as well, choking back a sob at the thought that it was all I had left. The over-the-counter diarrhea medicine that I had in my purse was counted and placed in an envelope for storage behind the nurse's station. I expressed concern, as I had been taking it frequently, but my worries were dismissed with a reminder that the staff would handle my medical needs.

Once the material items were dispatched, we moved on to a check of my physical state: no cuts, or injuries. I was given the rules of the house, which mainly covered liability on their part, and the privacy of the other patients. As long as I followed their rules, kept up with their schedule, and participated in all of the group activities, I would stay on the good side of the electronically sealed security door to my left and out of the seclusion area behind it. I nodded silently and slightly. I didn't have the will to live, so I certainly lacked the will to fight.

My host broke with the formality and gave me a pitiful look as he reached out and patted the back of my hand.

"You'll be okay, Ronnie. Okay?" I wanted to believe him, but I didn't. As I lay on the stiff mattress between strangely cold white sheets that night, I wondered if I could ever be okay again.

Living in a ward like that affords one a unique opportunity to experience how others deal with pain. Everyone there has made some kind of error in life, and that common background being a given in any conversation accelerates familiarity. We all had to take medication and adjust the side effects, and we were all locked inside. There was little left to do, but talk to one another and smoke cigarettes all day.

We often joked about the prison-like quality of the cigarette inside St. Joe's. Anyone who had contact with the outside through a family member or a friend had an obligation to use them in a courier capacity. It was an unspoken code. My parents sent me cartons of cigarettes in the mail, but I was subsidized on the inside before that. I was somewhat popular with the older folks—in particular, a giant of a man that we all dubbed "Papa Bear."

Papa Bear was a bipolar that fell for the "feel good" trap and stopped taking his medication. He was very kind and paternal, and had a great relationship with his wife in spite of his problems. She visited often, sharing meals with him. She usually brought me cigarettes and candy. I enjoyed the position of mascot, complete with free psychotherapy among the members of the group. They all had tales to share, as did I.

My closest circle of friends included Gina: an obese diabetic woman who was a former prostitute, crack-addict, and sometime mother with a rage disorder. She was a fundamentally nice person whose circumstances led her to become very gruff and hardened as a defense. Her former mate had abducted their daughter and arranged for her to be locked inside the ward to prevent chase. He was also her pimp and dealer—so much for sympathy for the father. She carried around drawings done by her little girl, and treasured the photos she still had tucked into a worn vinyl wallet photo case (sans wallet). Nothing made her happier than speaking to her little girl and nothing filled her with rage like something keeping her from the girl. The worst rage I had witnessed from her was directed at the counselor who disconnected the phones for group therapy time while Gina was talking to her child. She had to be pried from the nearly unconscious man by four other staff members to keep her from choking him to death.

Then, there was Julie. Julie's age was only speculation to most, but it was greater than mine was by at least a decade. She wore a thick, pasty mask of Joker-like cosmetics at all times, with layers of mascara that transformed her eyelashes into a single black flap. Her accent was heavily New York Jew, and her laugh was Vaudevillian in all respects. Julie was, at one time, an accomplished stage dancer before a drunk-driving accident left her with deformed knees and terrible pain. The ensuing addiction to pain killers led to chronic depression. Julie had a heart of gold-plated copper, which was severely damaged in her repeated shock therapy treatments. She desperately wanted attention from the opposite sex, and usually directed this desire at her psychiatrist. He looked like the King of Siam.

We smoked all day long, with intervals for the scheduled recreational, group, or educational therapy sessions. It was our only permitted vice, as they deprived us of caffeine and carbonated beverages.

After a few days of cocooning inside the protection of the ward, I decided to attend to business by calling the people I dealt with when I was sane. I notified my school of the illness and got a leave of absence, as I did with my job. I was less successful in my dealings with Jason, who informed me that he was leaving and would not be home when I got out. I was devastated by the news, but more so when I called the bank. He had taken every penny we had, then more. My account was overdrawn.

When I was released, I went back to the home that had become my pressure chamber. The houseplants had died, and the kitchen had been almost completely stripped. The television, the VCR, and anything else he could carry were gone. In a sense, he starved me into reconciling three months later. I clung to life alone for as long as I could, and lost touch with all else—including my sanity—until circumstances had beaten me into submission. I needed someone to stabilize me, and Jason was more than willing to come back in the guise of serving that role.

The joy of having him back in my bed was short lived. I was unemployed, without focus, and still suffering regular anxiety attacks and night terrors. The only thing that would save me, at that point, would be for me to adhere to a regular routine. He had other plans.

Within a few days of moving back into the apartment, Jason quit his job. He just stopped going. Suddenly his schedule consisted of sleeping all day, and playing video games all night. The nebulous fear that had been controlling me for months became so acute that my stomach would clinch and my chest would tighten at the thought of having to climb the stairs and go to bed alone. Viscerally, I was certain that I would never see him again. Pavlov would have been so proud. To avoid the nausea, I tried to stay awake as long as possible. Inevitably, I would slump over on the wood-frame futon that, along with a poorly supportive air mattress, was serving as our couch. I would doze uneasily until mid-morning, when I begged until Jason agreed to go to bed. This schedule did not allow time to look for a job.

When I was awake, I was in a state of constant panic. Sleep was an unfriendly territory full of darkness and intangible demons. Nightmares caused me to wake abruptly, gasping with a muted scream rattling in my chest. I worried about everything at once: the bills, the rent, the car, getting a job, getting my medication, getting cigarettes, and affording to eat. Eating was of a lesser priority for me, since the ward doctor added an anti-convulsive to my medical regimen. The doctor said it would help me control the bipolar illness, but all it did was make me panicky and anorexic. I had lost about 25 pounds since I started taking it, yet I was terrified to stop. I was terrified of everything, it seemed. The underlying horror of my life was punctuated by outbursts of crying and ranting about the impending doom. I would shake and sweat, and paw at Jason for comfort. He usually told me to sleep, and just forget it about it. Usually.

Eventually, he switched tactics for handling my attacks. When I began to cry, he would yell at me, threatening to leave me if I didn't stop. He would shake me by the shoulders and shout at me, telling me to shut up and drop it. He punched a hole through the door, implying that I would be next. Our roles were set in this precedent, and I was in no condition to fight it. I was lucky to have him back, and I had to behave in an agreeable manner if I wanted to keep him. I believed every bit of that, implicitly.

I finally gathered the strength to get out of bed, dress, and force myself to do what I had not been able to do for months: leave the house unaccompanied. When asked later, I attributed the strength I found to prayer. For the second time in a year, I found my only solace from insanity in the belief that God was a force that lived inside of me; I spoke to Him and He would never let me fail. It was a process of self-affirmation, acknowledging that my truest being wanted to live and thrive. Whatever happened, it still was true that I managed to lift myself out of the hell that I was living and make my way to a temporary job placement agency. Ultimately, I found a full-time job there, and being among the living again gave me life.

However, the roles were defined between Jason and me. I was playing the part that he chose for me, and it took me nearly a year—until my 29th birthday—to decide that I didn't want to play anymore.

Jason was suffering from respiratory distress due to what we believed to be high mold growth in the ventilation ducts of our filthy basement apartment. At his request, I stopped smoking in his presence; however, he continued to smoke. I didn't bother to protest the double standard, though. Any protests from me fell on deaf ears, whatever the subject, when he was in his best mood. The constant illness had left him weary, and the treatment—oral steroids—had turned the angry man into a despot.

We engaged in constant, irrational arguments about trivial things. His hateful attitude spared no living creature that crossed his path. Living with him was like being locked outside in a hailstorm. I grew tired of my own passive silence, and soon the arguments escalated into bouts of furniture throwing—such as the untimely demise of our office chair following my criticism of the way he treated the children in our apartment complex.

We lived in a gated community, and the gate was very slow to open. Frequently, pedestrians of all sorts used the larger, vehicle gate to enter the property because the pedestrian gate was broken or blocked. Drivers, as a result, had to wait a few extra seconds to enter the complex parking area. Jason didn't like to wait for anyone. One day, he rolled down the window and let a group of elementary school-aged kids know what he thought of waiting.

"Move! You bunch of fucking chili-choking sons of bitches! Fucking border jumpers!" He yelled loud enough for them to hear him clearly: them, and their families, and the other neighbors. I was mortified.

In retrospect, I probably should not have called Jason a fucking bigoted racist bastard. Nevertheless, I did, and the shouting match that began in the parking lot that afternoon ended in broken furniture that evening. When he picked up the chair, I was almost certain he was going to throw it at me. Instead, he hurled it into the floor with a frustrated growl, and proceeded to shake a meaty index finger at me, all the while flexing and stretching the fingers of the hand at his side. The memory of the door with the fist-hole in it became clearer in my mind, and I grabbed my keys and left for a few hours. He didn't try to stop me.

The final bout for me came in December, on a Sunday. Life was moving along peacefully, and we were getting along fairly well. We were both standing in our very cramped bedroom, on opposite sides of the bed, when Jason asked if I had seen his green shirt. Since he had more than one, I asked him to specify.

"Which green shirt do you mean?" I replied.

For reasons that are still a mystery to me, all hell broke loose at that moment.

Jason was enraged, and I refused to back down and cower because I felt that I had not done any wrong. For every insult and attack he delivered, I had a counter, or a parry. The yelling across the room progressed to closer range in the kitchen, then nose-to-nose in the dining room. Jason threw a damp washcloth into my face with as much force as he could muster at such a short distance, and made menacing gestures with his fists while he screamed into my face. I had backed into a desk.

As I have said, the guy was at least twice my size. He had been capable of horrible violence in his past, and wore a black teardrop tattoo on his hand with a cross to commemorate it. I had a sudden desire to avoid getting hit, and all defiance evaporated. I was more than scared.

Being a woman who had friends that had escaped abusive relationships, I had heard all of the hospital stories. Hell, I had seen my father toss one of his wives by the hair, like a doll. I did what society taught me to do. I called the police.

I told Jason, "You stay away from me, or I swear to God, if you don't kill me, I will kill you. I'm calling the police, so if you touch me..." I was dialing the phone, and listening in slow motion to the ring, "They can come here to break up a fight, or to bag up a body. It's up to you." I was bluffing and about to urinate all over myself in fear. I'd angered him more, and I knew I couldn't overpower him—but he was yelling at me from six feet away, instead of nose-to-nose.

By the time Phoenix's finest arrived, he was all goodness and light. I actually heard him tell the female officer, look at her, she's crazy! I hated him so much that I wished I had killed him.

We didn't bounce back from that confrontation. Not really. I couldn't live another lifetime with the threat of violence ever-present, so I had to leave.

My first step was to make sure the proverbial center would hold, and that required a subtle tweak of the medication. I contacted a clinic that specialized in mental health care.

Rather than getting involved with yet another medical doctor who dabbled in psychiatry, I went straight for the specialists. I didn't feel that I needed anything beyond medication maintenance, so I chose a psychiatric nurse practitioner named Cathy. She shared my view regarding fixing things that aren't broken (you don't), so we decided to continue the lithium dose I had been taking. We also decided that I should continue not taking the anti-convulsive. She threw in some wonder as to why I even took it in the first place. I appreciated that sentiment.

It took two months to settle on a supplemental anti-depressant to get me back on my feet after dealing with Jason's constant browbeating. Once that was done, I was able to rely on the support of my friends at work, my work, and my need to stretch myself spiritually to stay motivated toward the goal of leaving.

I turned to writing in order to help sort out the mess in my mind. I wrote an electronic journal entry one night that summed up the despair for me so well, that when I read it now, I recall my life with photo clarity. The negative absolutes of depression are present, along with a struggle to break out of a cycle of destruction.

11/12/01 10:09 PM Saturday

Another shitty weekend. We fight every time we have a few hours that we have to spend together. Every single weekend, the same thing happens. It's gotten to the point that I look forward to the weekend as a child looks forward to going home after getting suspended from school. I feel all of that same dread—as if I were heading for a punishment.

Usually, it turns out that I am being punished. I do everything wrong—too slowly, too sloppily, whatever. I felt that same sort of caged animal sensation before. I knew then that I was in trouble perpetually, no matter what I did. I developed a state of vigilance from learning numbness to constant guilt. I am always wrong. It doesn't really matter what I do.

The first time I felt this way, I was living with my stepmother. She was physically and verbally abusive. There was no discernible pattern for the abuse. I could be doing just about anything and I would find myself cowering under a hail of fists and angry epithets. The slightest transgressions earned disproportionately violent reactions. I was afraid even to breathe, and that is not hyperbole.

Therefore, I find myself reliving the same fear, shame, and guilt. I have never developed a healthy self-esteem. A healthy self-image was one luxury of childhood that was forsaken me. It gets no better in the current relationship. I am the target of constant criticism, yelling, hatred. The only time we seem to be close is when I am performing sexually.

And it is rarely my choice. That is not a marriage. It is a lie. That is what I am living.

I am an adult, but I do not have the ability to choose what I do in my free time. I really don't get free time. We spend every moment that we are not working together, and most of that time we are at each other's throats like pit bulls. I have been pushed, bruised, threatened, and emotionally battered on different occasions. Every weekend starts the same: I get out of bed, clean the house for four or five hours and still have to report when he comes home. Cook dinner, clean clothes, run errands. I don't relax on the weekend. The tension gets worse.

I started taking an anti-depressant a month ago. It was supposed to stop the fighting. (As always with this relationship, the only thing wrong with the two of us is me.) I take a drug twice a day to stifle the urge to kill myself each time it becomes clear that I am locked into a loveless, codependent relationship with no hope of reconciliation and repair. My sins are never forgiven, and my pain is never forgotten. The drugs are not solving the problem.

So now, I am left in a lucid state, wondering what will become of me. I dread being at home. I feel cheated in that I spend my time with a person that I cannot possibly communicate with on a normal level. We have no common ground, and disagree vehemently about many things. He has no respect for my health, or me or any sense of fairness and equity in the relationship. He smokes, and while that is not a big deal, it is a fine example of how shitty his regard for me is.

He has been sick for months. Asthma: it woke us both up several nights per week. I had to arrange medical care for him, and the doctor left us feeling desperate. He took steroids that made him even more angry and cruel. Menacing. That's how I described it to the police when they came to the house a few weekends back. I am hopeless and drowning in despair, and he is angry—very angry. He started to nag me about my smoking. I had to leave the house to smoke, couldn't smoke in the car—the usual. I committed to quit smoking to save his health. I had no desire to quit smoking; on the contrary, I was enjoying it. I knew I had to stop for his health. I quit—cold turkey, no patch, or gum. I stopped smoking because I knew I had to. It was not easy this time around. Of course, one of the things that made it harder was the fact the he was still smoking. Smoking in the house, and in the car. Putting cigarettes in my face. He sneaks, buying packs of cigarettes and keeping them at work. Wasting money. Cheating me out of our bargain—and enjoying the vice that I sacrificed in his name. Typical: Loveless, cruel, and inconsiderate.

Therefore, I look forward to the workweek. The only time that I am treated with any respect or value is when I am at work. The kindness there creates a serious imbalance with the side of the scale that my marriage rests on. Everyone treats me with respect and dignity. I am valued, and my opinion matters. The small things I do receive notice and thanks. I can be funny, witty, efficient, and smart. I matter. I find it abysmally sad that I have to turn to practical strangers to find the emotional fulfillment that I can't find at home. My friends are there, at my job. Not at home.

I was talking a few days ago, explaining how hard it is for me to get up and face every day. How I often consider the option of taking every single pill in every bottle, locking the door in the bathroom, and lying down in a warm bath forever. I don't do such a thing because I know two things: it wouldn't surprise anyone, as that is what has been expected from me since I was 12 years old, and no one would really get the point. They would have to care, first. If I say something like that at home, I get the usual shrug and advice to take my medication. As I said, no one is very surprised or concerned at home. At work, the shrug comes with a simple statement: "Don't do that. I would have no one to talk to, and that would suck. I would care." So glib a response, and at the time, I just laughed. But it matters. It matters because someone in the world who has no reason to makes me feel like I matter. My friends.

I don't know what to do, anymore. Being at home makes me feel like I don't really like being me. I don't get the feeling that I will live happily ever after in a marriage that supports the center of my life. I can't see myself growing old happily and looking back on all of the problems with a disbelieving shake of my head. I certainly don't see me sharing that exact moment with my equally aged husband who stood by me for the long years. What we share is a living space. There isn't much else. Discontent, perhaps.

I always hear that everyone fights. All couples have fights. I find it hard to believe that couples fight as bitterly and often as we do, and still stay together. If there were any love left, we wouldn't treat each other as we do. The cruelty would not be so sharp. If there were any happiness left, we wouldn't spend our time together so wastefully. Staying so separate from each other and speaking so critically. People who are happy do not sit and cry, and wait for it to just end. They don't feel buried under the knowledge that it won't end soon enough.

We shouldn't be married. We were separated—he left—and I was miserable. I was insane, at the time, and desperate for someone to save me from my madness. I called my parents several hundred miles away, begging for someone to let me lie in bed with the blankets over my head, and for that someone to take care of me. I regressed to four years old, in tears, and frightened. I couldn't take another day of loneliness, grief, and anxiety. As I unraveled on the phone, I heard the disgust in my father's voice. His frustration got the better of him. I knew I was completely lost. In the months, I had tried so hard to get accustomed to the notion of living alone. I imagined my life in solitude, visiting my friends, having a quiet social life. But the drama of my life overwhelmed me. I was reaching out for anyone who could save me from drowning in insanity. I called him and begged him to come back to me. He came, but the price that I have had to pay for that act of kindness and charity is that I had to be the weaker one—the needy one.

He took full advantage of the privilege of being the one who was called. If I spoke out of turn, if I cried, if I shouted, or whined, he would threaten to leave me. I had several days of crippling anxiety, where my fear would leave me weeping constantly. To compound that horrible fear, he would threaten me to shut up or he would leave. It was not much of a motivator. I was left screaming in horror inside myself, afraid to turn to anyone for help.

He did help, many times. I suppose he saved my life. I feel like I owe my current success to his support and care of me. I think the only draw for him was the feeling of being needed. Now, that is all over. There is nothing left for him to do, but to hate me. And I feel the need considerably less. We kid ourselves, and live in denial. Every day, I encounter something that brings back all of the pain of him leaving me. I can't seem to heal the million little wounds of my recent past. I can't move forward, and he does not lend a hand to lift me there.

We fight every time we have a day together. I don't want to go on with this. I know that I am destroying my life every day I live with this feeling of deep self-hatred. I waste my life to live in fear and anger. I don't know if we can repair the damage between us, or if we really want to. We are making such a splendid effort to hold on to our pain and use it against each other. It is a Promethean cycle of destruction and re-growth that has no apparent end. I can predict the finale.

Things are spinning away from the center, now. The time will come when the slamming door never opens again. I will take my own life, he will kill me, or we will both waste away in silent torture. The situation looks grim. Even more so, now, colored with the cowl of dark depression and tearful anger. These words have been in my head for months, now. I wish I could make a record of every time the pain comes, so that I could remember this sort of morbid clarity. When it finally comes to an end, however it does, I will be able to say that I saw it coming. If I am not around to say so, at least someone will be able to understand what I live in.

The few weeks I spent with Jason before my new apartment was ready were a true test of my will to live for myself, and stop serving the needs of others to my own detriment. I was doing my best to remain civil, and offered my future friendship as a consolation, but he continued to deteriorate emotionally. Oddly enough, when he wasn't bogged down in the mire of self-pity, he was bickering and dickering over the smallest possessions in the house. I became peeved, reminding myself that only my freedom mattered. He reminded me, too.

"Come on, Jason! You're keeping the VCR, the DVD player, and the microwave," I protested, "Why can't I have the portable CD player?"

"Hey, you are the one that's leaving. If you want it, you should stay." That had become his usual retort.

"It's not worth it. Keep it," I did my best to temper myself. "You bought it with my money. Consider it a gift."

I left there with little more than my own clothing, a few pots and pans and kitchen utensils, my bed, and a green recliner that had belonged to my father when he lived in his first house away from my mother. I took solace in the fact that the move would be easy. I didn't have the money or the manpower amongst my friends to handle a big move.

Chapter Two: Moving Out, Moving On

Jason and my friend, Dave, loaded up the moving truck that May morning, while I supervised and provided lunch. It didn't take long, and I was grateful that Jason spared me the waterworks. I wasn't sure I wanted to deal with that in addition to the logistics of the move.

My ground floor apartment made the unloading process even easier than the loading had been. Dave and I piled everything in the living room, except the bed. It all fit. By the time the sun went down, I was alone in my own place: the first, ever, that I didn't share with another person. The radio I bought in my twenties before I met Jason (and therefore got to keep) provided an accompaniment while I organized my meager belongings into a home.

The days passed quickly as I adjusted to the extra commute to work, and the duties of decorating my apartment in a manner that pleased the only person who mattered: me. Well, myself, and the pet lizard I kept in a small tank in the living room. I had to have some sort of companion, and was abundantly pleased with the silent, low-maintenance version.

I had started smoking again, but chose to do so outside for reasons of cleanliness. I had a great patio, overlooking a park full of old trees and busy families of starlings, pigeons, doves, and the occasional woodpecker. I spent more time in reflection in a plastic chair, staring up at my patch of sky, than I did smoking. I found it to be therapeutic.

Jason continued to contact me with various ruses. I didn't mind sharing a meal with him on occasion, or watching a movie. I didn't have a movie player of any kind, so I had no other way to fulfill my desire to watch my favorite films. I didn't have very much food, either, since he kept what we had. I didn't want to make a habit of it, however, so I declined a number of pleading invitations. Then, he began to discover belongings of mine that had been overlooked, and I would have to drop by to pick them up. On one occasion, he needed help with the computer, because it was "acting funny." I begrudgingly agreed to repair it.

The computer was a major point of contention in our property distribution for numerous reasons. At first, he said he would let me take it. A few days before I was set to leave, he changed his mind, leaving me with no connection to the outside world, no word processing, no games, and no way to play movies or any of the digital copies of the albums that he chose to keep. I was in disbelief that he would do something so crass—even more so because he knew little or nothing about using and maintaining a computer while I was working in information technology. Besides all of that, Floyd purchased the computer on his own credit, and gave it to us so I could go to school. It should have been paid for, but I offered to cover any remaining debt after we divorced.

"Well, you know how he feels about you for what you did to me," Jason reasoned, "and he told me he wanted the computer back before he'd let you have it. So I better keep it."

Mentally, I laid a ginger hand over the hole that was torn in my life when my dear Floyd yelled at me on the phone in my weakest moment. I had no argument or willpower to argue against that.

I drove over to his place—formerly, our place—after work, and set to diagnosing the problem. Jason had moved the computer into the bedroom and created an office to fill the space where the bed had been. He was sleeping on the futon—a fact I did not pity, since I had, only a few months prior, dropped an entire paycheck on the best quality mattress and cover for the thing. I had coveted the Asian embroidery design that I had specially ordered to cover the mattress.

While I worked on the computer, he filled the background with a rambling litany of pathos. He droned on about how lonely he was, and how he was looking for work, and a new apartment, but he wasn't having much success. He had no one to talk to, and though he considered talking to Floyd, he wasn't sure how to admit to him that we had actually reunited, much less that we split up again. I remembered how much Floyd hated me, didn't I? What a dilemma.

I was reliving the guilt I felt when Floyd yelled at me as I investigated his computer problems. I wandered upon a folder in the file structure that was unusually large, jam-packed with photos: snapshots, taken casually, of a girl with badly bleached hair sitting in provocative poses with a motorcycle, or sharing cleavage with her friends in a bar, surrounded by half-consumed glasses of beer. There were twenty or thirty of these gems, along with saved chat files that were of the less tasteful variety. I knew I had been duped into pitying his loneliness. I was livid, and made my exit promptly.

I viewed my reaction to his pranks as a weakness. I was trying to seek a center of happiness in myself, and to control my temper. I let him get the better of me, and I didn't want to do it again. I swore to myself, that I would stop letting him damage me. I would become the person I needed to be and let karma deal with Jason. Unfortunately, Jason wouldn't let me.

Near the end of June, I received an email from Jason's mobile phone, simply asking me to come outside and talk to him. He was waiting for me near the car that I'd been suckered into helping him buy, leaning against the hood. I was still fighting the instinct to treat him hatefully in the hope that I could better myself, so I smiled as I greeted him. He hugged me, and lit a cigarette.

He then proceeded to deliver a tale to me that I had never expected—but should have. He had been coughing a great deal with the effects of his asthma and allergy season. The week before, he coughed so hard that he lost consciousness for a few hours, and noticed that he had been coughing up blood. He went to the emergency room, and they took a chest x-ray and gave him a breathing treatment with Albuterol. The x-ray showed an abnormal mass which, upon further study by the doctors at the Scottsdale Mayo Clinic, turned out to be a cancerous growth. Because of the position on the bronchus, it was inoperable. Because of the size of the mass, it was life threatening. The type of growth—non-small cell, differentiated carcinoma—made it rapidly terminal. He was not expected to see his next birthday, his 30th, in February.

I was concerned, of course. Being raised by my father, who is an experienced nurse, led me to react clinically. Had they done a biopsy? Was he considering chemotherapy? I suggested that he should consider skipping chemical or radiation treatments if they weren't going to help, so that he could maintain a higher quality of life. I advised him to go home, immediately, and see his family. I suggested that he talk to Floyd. Floyd had worked as an Oncology nurse for years, administering chemotherapy to patients. Floyd would know what his real options were.

He dismissed all of these things, saying he just wasn't sure what to do. I offered, in light of this new situation, to consider hastening or delaying the divorce process, depending on what would be best for us both. I suggested that the divorce could wait a while, if it would help. He agreed, and said that he didn't know how to tell anyone else, so he wanted to talk to me. He said he'd be in touch.

When I returned to work, I was obviously shaken, and was led outside to take a walk by my friend, Corrine. I fell apart as I told her what I'd learned, sobbing. I must have passed through all of the stages of grieving at a pace of one minute each. Ultimately, I blamed myself. I knew that I had wished him dead on more than one occasion, and I was sure that Jason's cancer was the culmination of my hatred.

"Oh, I'm sorry. I didn't realize you were all-powerful." Corrine was deliciously blunt when you needed it—and sometimes, when you didn't. "You did not give Jason cancer, okay? I would place more blame on his years of smoking cigarettes."

"And weed, and crystal meth," I added, sniffling.

"Yes. He did this to himself, not you." She was great for tough love. "So, what are you going to do? Go back? "

There was no way in hell I was going back. I could be his friend, and attend his funeral, but the days of being his wife were long over—and I liked it that way. I told her so, and she agreed.

"Are you sure he's really got cancer? Did he show you proof, or anything? "

I told Corrine that I could not possibly imagine that he would make something like that up. Firstly, because that was just too horrible, and secondly, because I didn't think he was smart enough to come up with the terms he used to describe it. That's what I told both of my parents, as well, after they stopped celebrating his impending demise. My parents never liked Jason, or the way he treated me.

My friends were divided nearly evenly on the topic of whether I should go back to Jason and be the caring hospice wife. I had veto power, though, and I wouldn't do it. I told everyone who opposed me that it was simple, really: he was dying, but I was not. I didn't want to stunt my life by sitting around, waiting for him to die. He wouldn't have done it for me.

Regardless, I continued to help him whenever he needed me, and I pitied him. I spent time with him, socially, and I helped him move in to his new apartment because I felt that I owed it to him. The endless droning about his loneliness continued, though I knew it was a lie. One girlfriend showed up unannounced while I was there, eating dinner. He shooed her away from the door, comically.

I moved on, re-entering the dating world. My sessions with Dr. Santo had evolved into a strange sort of confessional as I recounted my sexual exploits, looking for meaning. He never judged me, and I loved him for that—at least, I thought he was worth my time and money.

He didn't let me get away with scurrying back into my self-loathing. He didn't let me get away with anything, period. I have a great deal of respect for those who are clever enough to catch me bullshitting. I feel like that is a quality I will always require of a therapist. If I am fighting my way through the underbrush of unreality and self-deception, I need a guide who is not afraid to cut through the nonsense. I need someone who is does not hesitate to say that the Emperor has no clothes.

I went through a brief period in which I was struggling to create a relationship out of a very brief affair with an obese, unemployed, elitist frat-boy type. I was absorbed in the melodrama, and the good doctor knew it. I told him I'd been listening to a Chet Baker tune as of late, and I thought it would make an appropriate theme for me.

"Chet Baker? Which song? No! Wait," he rose and walked over to his shelf, then to a boom box on his desk. A few clicks later, my song was wafting from the speakers.

He handed me the case as he returned to his chair. The Best of Chet Baker, with a black and white photo of a young man and his trumpet on the front, and my song listed as track 3: "I Fall in Love Too Easily." I was aghast, and I could not believe the odds that my doctor would have this CD in his office. I nodded. That was my song, and those were my words, coming out of the young Chet Baker's talented mouth in his baby-sweet voice:

> *I fall in love too easily*
> *I fall in love too fast*
> *I fall in love too terribly hard*
> *For love to ever last*
> *My heart should be well schooled*

*'Cause I've been fooled
In the past
But still I fall in love too easily
I fall in love too fast*

Dr. Santo sat, deep in thought, listening to the silken tones and brush-cymbal siren of jazz lounge at its finest. Suddenly, he crumpled the bridge of his nose and squinted his eyes in a look of negation.

"Nope," he turned off the music, "I think you should probably find a better song."

"I can't help it," I whined childishly, "I always do it. I always fall for these guys who don't want me or need me. I love to be in love."

He sat back in his chair, cocked his head to the side as if to hear better, and said, "Don't bring that weak shit in here. You know better. Let's try that again."

How does one resist such leadership? I straightened myself out immediately, and resigned myself to be honest, after that—out of general respect for the man. It was the best policy for both of us, after all. If I was honest with him, I was straight with myself, and that is the path to fixing one's damage.

My greatest breakthrough with Dr. Santo came on a day when the session lacked its usual direction. This is something we did, on occasion: we would just talk, converse, like normal people. Every appointment, I would leave with an assignment of sorts, a behavior that I should observe, or a feeling that I should note in detail when it occurred. When I returned, we would dedicate the beginning of the appointment to discussing what I had learned. More often than not, I would have forgotten what I was supposed to have learned, so, we'd just talk.

I was involved in a dead-end relationship with yet another misfit; the difference this time was that the guy was treating me pretty well. I simply refused to believe that he had any real interest in me. I explained this to Dr. Santo adding that it wasn't that I thought the guy was any better than I was—on the contrary—he was socially inept.

"What, then?" Dr. Santo urged the conversation forward, though I was stammering in an effort to formulate the real problem clearly for him.

"I don't know," I waved my hands exasperatedly, "I guess if I don't have someone nagging me all the time, I think they just don't care about me."

He sat up in his chair with a grin, and I froze in my seat with an expression on my face as though someone had just slapped me. He was holding his pen in mid-air, over his notepad.

"Please. Please repeat that." He was rapt. "We really ought to write that down."

I repeated it, and the words felt foreign in my mouth: stiff, like cardboard. I could barely believe that such a simple thing had never occurred to me. I was calling the demon by name, and I had only to cast it out. I was on a roll.

"That's not love!" I was angry, and I felt that I had been cheated for years. "Nagging and verbal abuse: that's not love! What the hell—how did I get like this? "

I gave that question a great deal of contemplation when I got home. How in the name of all that is holy? How did I get like this?

CHAPTER THREE: THE POWERS THAT BE

When I was fifteen years old, my father sat with me on the edge of my bed, and talked to me with a sort of candor that can be achieved only through consuming copious amounts of alcohol. He told me a story of my mother that I had not heard before—which was unusual for my dad. I'm not sure if he was trying to prove that he had always been there for me, or that he'd always been the only one who cared about me. I wasn't sure whether anything he said was designed to make me feel better, but it didn't.

My father was the only son of an only son. He was the last hope for the family line, and as such, felt a great need to carry on the family name. His first marriage had been a matter of myth to me, and little more than a brief lapse of judgment on his part in the post-Vietnam era. I assumed that, once he'd gotten the family jewels home in one piece, he wanted them in a safe-deposit box as soon as possible. I couldn't fault him for that, even though he was married to his fourth wife and looking for a fifth at the time of our conversation.

I had been complaining that my recently shorn hair left me looking like my mother, and he had agreed. It is a tragic thing for children to know their parents are hated—who else in the world should be thanked for our creation, in that case? As I hated her more than most, I took no pleasure in ever being compared to her.

He would hear none of it. "Your mother was one of the most beautiful women I had ever seen," he confessed. "Even after I got away from her, I thought she was beautiful. Nuts," he laughed, "but beautiful."

I had never heard a good word about that woman, and I wasn't sure how to take it. He continued, ever painting himself as the portrait of a saint. I don't doubt that my father tried to be a good man, but I am sure there was a touch more fallibility to his past.

In his tale, he met my mother and was completely smitten. He did all he could to show his love for her, and when he married her, he adopted her two children. He even changed the boy's middle name to be the same as his, so he would feel that he belonged. This would be my schizophrenic sister, Annie Jean, who was eight years my senior, and my big brother, Willie, who was six years older.

Now suddenly, Ronald Schiller had a beautiful wife and two small kids at 25 years of age. He wanted to bring it all together, to create a unified family. In other words, he wanted his beautiful wife to have his baby. He asked, begged, pled with her for a year, but she refused. At last, she gave her acquiescence under one condition:

"She said, 'you give me a house, and I'll give you a child'," my father told me. "So I had them start building that house in Wickliffe."

Magically, on Ron Schiller's 26th birthday, I was conceived. My mother kept up her end of the deal, delivering an offspring. In exchange, she got a redbrick ranch-style house in the best neighborhood in Wickliffe, with a big picture window in the front. When I was born, my father was so proud, despite his need for a boy to ensure the Schiller lineage. He had picked out a name for me that would embody all the beauty of a woman: Brigitte Marie, after the famous French actress, Bardot. He raced to the phone in the hospital lobby to call his parents, and deliver the good news of my arrival. Brigitte Marie Schiller was born!

My mother had plans of her own, and while my father was singing his triumph to the family, she was filling out the birth certificate. When the beaming new daddy returned to the room, she held my sleeping body out to him.

"Here's your kid, Ron." She rolled over as much as she could away from him, calling over her shoulder, "Her name is Ronnie. She's all yours."

The earliest memories I have are of my father. At the time, he was little more to me than a pair of towering white-clad legs and a friendly face framed in shiny black hair. I was not aware of the hours of the day, but I knew when he was home, because he always brought me a gift: a small teddy bear, a canister of Tinker Toys, or a book about a brown and white puppy. Daddy had a profound effect on me, because he was the only one who spoke to me all day.

My father was attending school to become a registered nurse while I was in the womb. After I was born, he worked several jobs to support me, and the rest of the family. He drove an ambulance, and worked in a hospital emergency room when I was a toddler; both jobs took him thirty or more miles away from home, for hours of the day and night.

My earliest memory of my mother comes later—I was around four years old. I was standing in the doorway to her bedroom, leaning my right shoulder on the frame, with my dingy yellow security blanket in my left hand—the thumb of which was poised in front of my mouth. My mother lay on her bed; face down and backwards, with her head near me. She was clothed, on top of the blankets, and her right foot was lodged in the recess of her gold velveteen cushioned headboard. In the crook of her curled arm was the telephone, and in her hand was a clear plastic bottle.

"Mommy? Mommy?" Each call to her grew in crescendo until my shouting attracted Annie Jean's attention. "MOMMY?"

Everything afterward was a blur. I knew that someone used the phone, and suddenly there were men in our small house, running down the hall to my parents' room with a rolling bed. I saw my daddy, and I wanted to run to him, but he was busy with the men, the bed, and my mother. I had to stand back as they took her away. She was sleeping, and then she was gone; not for good, though—just for a stay at the state hospital in Hopkinsville.

My father was not around much then, but he left us in good care. Jay Jones was my father's best friend in a class where men—heterosexual men—were scarce. In the early 1970s, nursing was largely a woman's job, as it typically is today, but more so. My dad, however, was sure he could do a better job than most of the women he'd seen. He did—and Jay did the same. Jay-Jay, as I called him, was one of my favorite people in my limited social scope of toddlerdom. He gave me the one companion who never hurt me—or anyone else that I can recall—a shaggy white mixed-breed mutt that I named "Joey" in an infantile effort to say his name. Jay-Jay also gave me the gift of a caring mother to look after me: his own mother, JoAnne.

JoAnne was a big, soft, round woman with thin gray hair and a broad face. She was quiet, and content to watch television while I played on the floor all day. She never raised her voice, and was always attentive to me. She was no Mary Poppins—she smoked menthol cigarettes too often, and would drive us crazy by rattling the ice in her plastic tumbler of Kool-aid, constantly—but I loved her. I would climb into her giant lap and giggle, taking drags of cool menthol vapor from an unlit cigarette until my lips tingled. It was a simpler time.

As my fifth birthday approached, JoAnne let me help her in the kitchen. She made the best chicken and dumplings I've ever tasted, and it seemed like she spent the entire day over the stove. She made a pie for my dessert—pistachio pudding pie—and I laughed hysterically at the opportunity to smash whole boxes of graham crackers for the crust by stomping the paper bag on the kitchen floor with enthusiastic vigor and solemn diligence. As a special reward, she heated up a can of mushrooms in butter and gave me the whole thing in a bowl. I loved mushrooms. Small gifts mean so much when they demonstrate intimate knowledge of the recipient.

My mother sent a loom-woven potholder that she had made, and a plaster bust of my father. It was painted with a dark brown ceramic glaze. I thought it was creepy, and was glad to see it put up on a shelf in the coat closet.

I spent the majority of the day playing with a train set my daddy gave me while JoAnne presided over the festivities with a cigarette from her place on the couch. He took me out to play pinball, which I loved despite the fact that my chin just grazed the tabletop if I stood on my toes. We wrapped the day with a ride on the coin-operated miniature carrousel outside GG's Burger Bar. GG's was not so much of a bar, as it was a booth slightly larger than a portable toilet with a built-in kitchen and room for one man to cook, serve, and take the money. It was all white and pale blue inside, and they served their banana splits in flimsy blue plastic boats, complete with molded wood grain. These little boats always met their demise in the bathtub, capsizing under the weight of a plastic wind-up seal with spinning flippers. We took home one more, that afternoon.

I remember feeling like the world was mine that day, getting so much attention from my father, and JoAnne, and sharing cake with Annie Jean and Willie—I got the biggest piece. Even though I could read and write letters and numbers masterfully by then, I had not been able to understand what was taking place in the world of the people who towered above me. I didn't know what my father's life was like, or why my mother was gone. I didn't know my parents were getting a divorce. I still thought my name was Baby. I had much to learn.

Then my dad left me. He never meant to, and he practically killed himself to see me when he could, but he still left me.

When my mother returned from the hospital, she seemed a bit more cheery. I am told that she was taking lithium to control her bipolar illness. Most of the time she left us kids alone with JoAnne, so her return was a ripple in the pond that really didn't move my figurative lily pad.

Shortly after her return home, weekend visitation with my father began. This commenced the ritual of stuffing two days' clothing in a paper grocery bag and sitting for two hours of commute each way that would continue for five years. That first trip provided me with a look at the woman who would be taking my mother's place on visitation weekend. She looked very different from my mother: short, stocky, blonde hair, and big breasts. She was younger than my mother was—which probably explained her nervous demeanor around Willie and me when we visited her apartment the first time. She acted like a woman who had never considered dealing with her lover's kids. I spent most of the weekend with my nose buried in a math-teaching toy shaped like a happy owl wearing a blue mortarboard.

I spent my preschool years at home. Once I was able, I would spend each weekday morning pressing my face against the picture window to watch Willie disappear up the street as he walked to school. Annie Jean was usually ahead of him, taking impossible strides with her long legs. The difference in our ages hampered the connection between us, regardless of the fact that we shared a room in the little house.

Willie had to order me to remain inside the house every day, promising that I would join them soon in going to school. My five-year old imagination transformed school into the greatest sort of treat. Sadly, when I began to attend school, I discovered a world outside of home where I did not quite fit. The thrill of walking to school with Willie faded when I had to struggle to keep my short legs in pace with his. Even though we were venturing farther from home without an adult than I had gone before, the sense of inadequacy tainted the adventure. I found myself a misfit in my class. Most of the other girls had neatly brushed and braided hair, sometimes with ribbons. I was more feral than that, after spending so much time in the yard with Joey as a playmate, or trekking through the woods. I wasn't the prettiest, or the smartest, or the fastest student. I was not Baby any more—at least, not there. I missed my yellow blanket.

I was released in the early afternoon, along with the other kindergarteners. The walk home from school was a much more leisurely affair for me than the race to arrive each morning. I would cut across the lower grades' playground, past the half-buried tractor tire and the seesaw, to the gap in the chain link fence. Most days, I would approach the fence posts with trepidation, and investigate the space reflexively for spider webs. On the occasion that I'd charge through without checking, I'd usually regret it with a close encounter with a banana spider or some other eight-legged menace. I imagined that the spiders built their webs in that spot, intending to feast on the delicious fluids of a hapless child.

The other side of the playground fence was occupied by Wickliffe's only funeral home. The split-level plantation home rested away from the road behind a broad lawn full of lush Kentucky grass, dotted evenly with dogwood trees. I always liked the look of the place, though I had no idea what purpose it served. The home's red bricks and black shutters contrasted regally with its white pillars. Moreover, the lawn was much larger than ours was and full of clover flowers for making garlands.

Continuing homeward, I passed an oddly located house. I never saw the people who lived there, but Willie told me they had a daughter his age that had a short, mangled arm because they didn't fix it correctly after she broke it. He said she was a nice girl.

A line of trees separated the property from a huge hollow in the earth, overgrown with kudzu and home to a thriving groundhog population. The locals referred to this area as "the gully." Thanks to the kudzu, the gully was a prime spot for stashing items such as six-packs of beer, cigarettes, or dirty magazines away from the view of parents and other authorities. In the spring and summer, the kudzu spread fingers covered with broad spade-like leaves over the entire sidewalk, but in the fall, it receded into the slopes of the gully as if repulsed by the chill. I had a nagging fear of falling into the gully and being lost, so I clung to the guardrail near the road when I passed it on the way to the street that wound down to my house.

Home was a little structure at the gravelly end of the street. Our house resembled every home ever drawn by children with crayons: a cube of maroon bricks with a slightly pitched black roof. One big window sat on the front, with a white door on the left, and a driveway on the right.

I would let myself in, and spend the afternoon curled in a ball, napping in the space behind JoAnne's folded legs on the couch. I woke instinctively from every nap in time to run up the street and meet Willie excitedly as he came home.

When I was in the first grade, both of my parents remarried. Mother, as I addressed her, married Scott. I didn't know where he came from, but he was a sweet young man—5 or 6 years her junior—who had never been married before. He was jolly and completely at ease with the kids. He even drove the school bus that transported the rural kids from the farming areas into Wickliffe to attend the elementary school. I thought he was the greatest, with his country-rock band practicing in the living room. JoAnne liked him, Mother seemed happy, and my dad even relaxed a little bit because he knew Scott would take care of me.

My dad married the little blonde, only to discover that she was a redhead. In time, we learned that my stepmother, Marcy, was scarcely as she seemed.

Marcy and my father bought a little red A-frame house, which I adored. I continued to visit him on the weekends, but Willie stopped coming after Marcy made him wait in the car while she introduced me to her parents. The move had taken them farther from Wickliffe—over fifty miles away—so most of the visit was spent in the car. Regardless, he never missed a weekend.

For a time, everything seemed to be placid. My comfort at home lent me the courage to venture outside and become acquainted with nature. I felt that I belonged in the woods, among the old oak trees and mosses. I felt un-pressured, and enjoyed the discovery of it all. I picked bunches of wild flowers and blackberries for no one, in particular, and came home in the evening with dark forest soil on my bottom and my knees. Nature would soon become my best and preferred escape, and the closest thing I had to God.

CHAPTER FOUR: HIDDEN BY A TREE

I've often heard people remark that children possess a sort of magical awareness, on a subconscious level, replete with an insight into the relationships of their caregivers. They just "know" what's going on. Rubbish.

I had no idea what my mother was doing. I didn't understand why Scott was crying, and walking out the door—or why my mother was feathering up her dyed black hair and caking white erase under her eyes before she went out. I noticed that she brought a strange man into the house, and they were dancing in the living room. They hid in her bedroom with the door locked.

She never even introduced her new husband to me, until the title was his. Then, I learned that the longhaired man in the bell-bottoms and square-toed shoes was Clifton Nunn. Not Cliff, mind you, but Clifton—always. His brother, Billy Boy, was the sixth grade teacher at my school—and the only gay man I knew of at age 7. He never openly admitted it, but with his strongly effeminate behavior and blue satin short-shorts, I think everyone knew something was different about him. Still, every year, Billy Nunn would take a group of boys to Disney World in Florida, and every year their parents gave consent. Willie even made the trip, once. He was trusted.

Shortly after Clifton moved in, JoAnne moved out. Mother made her leave, or Clifton did. As an adult, looking back, I cannot empathize with my mother to understand why she would expel the woman who cleaned our house and fed us. Perhaps she felt that JoAnne was an unwelcome spy for Daddy's army. She chose Annie Jean to take JoAnne's place—and the fifteen year-old, with her social issues and natural antipathy for all things familial, was a poor substitute. Before long, my diet consisted of steady helpings of free school lunch and bread with milk gravy.

My father informed me that he was fighting for my custody, but it was not going well. My mother was enjoying the benefits of my siblings' child support and mine. I wondered where she put it, because our refrigerator was empty. He also told me that Marcy was going to have a baby, and I was desperately excited to have a little brother or sister. I hoped he would win, so I could see the baby every day. Besides, home was getting to be a strange place.

The little brick house was designed inside as simply as it was outside. The front door, which bore a foot-sized hole in the middle from some years-old assault, opened on a living room with green sculpted carpet. There was a coat-closet to the left, and an open doorway across from the big window, to the right. The carpet was filthy with dog hair, food, and beer spills.

Through the open archway was the kitchen, with torn and peeling yellow, brown, and black starburst linoleum flooring. A square table on the right and a stackable green washer and dryer on the left mostly occupied the kitchen, with a stove, sink, and refrigerator clockwise toward the back door. A pile of trash with a heavily laden trashcan in its center frequently blocked this door, which opened onto the driveway. This mess was often home to maggots and other vermin, and accompanied by one or two paper bags stuffed with sour-smelling empty Bush beer cans—Clifton's favorite—for recycling.

Proceeding through the living room one would enter a narrow hallway, with more green carpet. The hall was not wide enough for two people to pass at the same time, and was paneled with the same black walnut paneling that covered the walls in the rest of the house, so that a hollow thump would issue from them if they were accidentally struck. Even more noise emanated from the hall closet on the left, with sliding wooden doors that hung swinging from the top tracks and free at the bottom. Directly across from the closet was Willie's room, which was little more than a white-plaster box with a window.

The purpose of the next room had exchanged repeatedly over the years with its counterpart across the hall. At that time, it served as my and Annie Jean's bedroom. We shared a queen-size bed, and a dresser, and a closet with no doors. The utility closet behind our door housed the water heater. Annie Jean—she was incredibly talented—had precisely painted a scene from Bambi on the door, and inside the door-less closet beside it. We had two windows: one facing the rear of the house, westward, and another facing the south side of the lot. By some magic of the slope of the lot, our windows were at a perilous distance from the ground. This played a role in Annie Jean and I getting this room—they were employed to keep her from sneaking out.

Across the hall was my mother's bedroom, with the same yellow-gold velveteen headboard as always. There were unfamiliar objects added to the room, including a small refrigerator stocked with beer, booze, and Mother's special foods that the kids couldn't touch, such as cottage cheese, fruit, and milk—the "expensive" food. There was a new color television with stolen cable service, a huge drip-candle sculpture, a black light poster of a ship called The Mary Jane, and a window-mounted air conditioner. That was the only means of cooling the house. I only glimpsed these items, though, because of the newest addition to Mother's room: a padlock, with a clasp on the inside for when she was home, and one on the outside for when she was not.

The little bathroom, which held the awful wall heater that burned me every time I bent over to dry my feet, was in the middle between the two rooms.

The tiny house was packed, more often since the wedding, with Mother's new friends who came to drink beer and play cards until they passed out on the kitchen floor or in bed with Annie Jean and me. In the morning, I would creep across the linoleum, collecting the coins that had been dropped during the card game, and then take the money to the Jiffy Mart to buy penny candy for breakfast. The house was perpetually strewn with beer cans and half-empty bottles of Maker's Mark (Clifton's brand). Cleaning up after the parties was as educational as it was arduous. I'll never forget the shock on my father's face when I told him about the roach I found in the living room ashtray.

It seemed that Annie Jean had less and less time, so Willie and I had to take care of each other. Mostly, he took care of me.

Willie had always been the reasonable one in the family. He took care of me, and taught me whatever he had learned at school, so I came to love learning. Though he was only six years older than I was, he cared for me, as a parent should have. Willie taught me how to tie my shoes, how to count to ten in Spanish, and how to fry bologna. When I was sick, Willie would have me stretch across the couch, and he would create an "animal blanket" for me. He found every stuffed animal, doll, and soft toy in the house, and tucked them all around my body on the couch until nothing but my face was showing. He would turn on the TV to keep me company and give me my yellow blanket before he left for school.

We'd play outside together when his friends were not available. We spent countless hours digging through the gravel of our driveway, searching for what he called "lucky rocks"—cylindrical pieces of rock that resembled fossilized sticks. We had a treasury of lucky rocks housed in glass soda bottles. Today, a lucky rock adorns my key chain.

Willie was still human, of course. He was still a big brother, and as such, performed all manner of sibling cruelties for which big brothers are renowned. There was the "AreYouGonnaCatchIt?" wherein he would tease me with a ball until I was near tears. Then he would act as if he were going to throw it to me, and instead, bounce it off my head and back into his own hands. There was also the Chant.

The Chant was mostly a gag for his neighborhood pre-teen buddies. It was born one afternoon when Willie's pals were all gathered in the backyard, watching a box turtle that had wandered out of the bushes. I wanted to see what was happening, even though I had seen box turtles before. I just wanted to tag along, which is worse than poison ivy for a boy and his pals. Somehow, I found myself in the middle of a circle of boys, being threatened with a curse if I didn't go away immediately. Since I didn't believe in curses (sort of), I persisted.

"Fine, then," Willie looked at the others, signaling them to play along.

They chanted, "Die, Baby, Die!" until I burst into tears and fled to the house, where I locked them out.

That was the best prank I knew.

My reliance on Willie reached its peak in the fall of that year. Annie Jean was afflicted with adolescence, which made it nearly impossible to talk to her. She was pretty, thin, and very tall for a girl (so I was told). I was also told that she had a bad reputation where boys were concerned. I'd heard about it on the small town playground. I wonder how bad she really was, now that I am older.

A friend of Mother's named Dan took Annie Jean to Colorado for Christmas break. Dan was a grown-up, and kind of creepy with a mustache and glasses. I didn't think much of it, at the time. After all, Billy Boy took Willie to Disney World. She returned with a t-shirt and stories about the snow.

A few days after her return, Mother and Clifton were throwing another party. Dan was there, along with the usual cast. I was told to go to bed, as were my siblings, so the grownups could play cards, shout, and drink beer in peace. We had been dozing in the dark room for a while, when the door opened. I could tell by the light coming through the window that it was Dan, but I didn't dare move. I pretended to be asleep. Moments later, he was having sex with my sister, and I was shoved out of the bed and onto the floor.

I was angry at how rude they were. I didn't know that I should be bothered by my mother's 34 year-old friend having sex with her 15 year-old daughter, probably with her consent. I needed a place to sleep. I stepped out into the dark hallway, and I began to cry, loudly. I was right in front of my mother's bedroom door, and I wanted her to yell at Annie Jean for what she had done. I sobbed, half yelling, but got no response. I took a pace or two toward the living room and elbowed the hall closet doors gently, then harder. No Mother.

A gentle voice raised itself in a loud whisper from the room in front of me.

"Come on, Ronnie," Willie called in disgust, "You can sleep in here. Forget about them."

For a while, I did just that. Sharing a room with Willie made the next year more fun, by far. When he had homework to do, he would learn by teaching me the lesson. I was learning middle school curriculum from a middle school point of view. I loved learning about Algebra, World Geography, and Spanish. The best part, though, was learning about Willie's literature homework and choir practice. The second grade provided nothing so interesting.

Every night, before I fell asleep, Willie would make a little puppet out of his hand and hold it up against the moonlight coming in the window. The puppet would sing choir songs: selections from "Oklahoma!" or odd little tunes, the favorite of which was "High Hopes." I would fall asleep feeling happy and secure, and wake up excited to recap the homework lessons on the way to the elementary school, where Willie caught a bus to the middle school.

About a month after my eighth birthday, Marcy gave birth to a boy, Brandon. I was thrilled to have a little brother, but Willie told me that my dad wouldn't want me since he had a new baby.

Especially considering that, I was just a girl. Of course, Willie also told me that I was adopted, and then that I was Polish and my real last name was Schillerski. He wasn't exactly reliable as source of information. Besides, the baby was beautiful, and he seemed to be crazy about his big sister, in the way that babies always like other kids.

Mother and Clifton continued to be the strangers that lived in the house with us. Clifton was working some sort of manual labor for the railroad, while Mother was working swing shift at a hospital across the state line in Illinois—she was an LPN. On the weekends, they drank and partied, or locked themselves in the bedroom all day. It was the normal way of life for us. I was a latchkey kid before they had a name for it.

Summer finally came along to end my second grade year. I was free to roam the woods, picking flowers, and catching every reptile or amphibian that I could to make it my pet. The blackberries were ripening and would soon fill my basket. Honeysuckle was fragrantly waiting to drop nectar on my tongue. For the first time, Annie Jean and Willie were leaving the house for two weeks to attend a college summer program for poor kids—and leaving me full access to the TV and the new Atari system. Willie was ecstatic about spending time in a dormitory on the campus in Murray. That was the reason he left me.

I spent most of my day outside, playing with Joey, or wandering alone. The Phillips family next door lived in a little green trailer, with beautiful flowers all around it and a vegetable garden in the back. Next to the garden, there was a thick old tree with a low limb like a bench. I would dawdle there and sing along with flocks of mockingbirds, pretending that I could understand them. I walked through all of the yards in the neighborhood, picking the blackberries that grew along the edge of the woods that surrounded our subdivision. There were no fences, and it didn't occur to me that the neighbors would care because no one ever said so.

Once the sun had made its exit, and the cicadas had begun to sing, I would head back to the house. I found it empty, with Mother at work and Clifton locked in the bedroom. I would make myself a (government) cheese sandwich, sometimes with pickles and mustard, and find a spot on the floor to watch TV until I became sleepy. It wouldn't take too long for the heat and humidity of a Kentucky summer night take over, especially since the only air conditioner was locked in Mother's bedroom.

One night, shortly after Willie and Annie Jean had begun their college adventure, Clifton came out to the living room and told me that I should come to his room and watch TV with him. This unexpected kindness made me feel special, as if I was in on a secret that no one else knew.

"Come on," he said as he headed back down the hall. "You can lie down in here where the air conditioner is."

The bedroom was the forbidden zone in the house, yet I was going inside. I climbed on the big bed and tried to look unimpressed by the small white refrigerator and the giant mound of rainbow-hued candle remains. I squinted in the semi-darkness at the posters. The TV was high on a shelf in the corner of the room—to the left of the bed. The only light in the room came from the television, and around the cracks of the sliding closet doors. I marveled that my mother's closet had a light inside. Immediately to my right, the air conditioner announced its importance with a loud hum.

Clifton was watching the college exploitation film, "H.O.T.S.," featuring the breasts of scores of young women and Danny Bonaduce from the daytime show I watched in re-run. I tried to be grown-up enough to watch it, and was impressed with myself that he would let me.

Soon, the darkness and the comfort of the room left me snoozing. At Clifton's suggestion, I had climbed into bed in my usual sleeping attire: a pair of cotton underpants. We did not place much value in modesty in my house. I curled in the fetal position, facing the closet and slept that way for an unknown amount of time. When I woke, I froze in place.

Clifton was humping me. He was naked, and I could feel him rubbing something hard against me. I tried to pull forward, but he was holding my hip. I craned my neck around, and his eyes were closed so I thought he might be dreaming. I made coughing noises to wake him, but he wouldn't stop. I pushed his shoulder and said "Wake up!" He still didn't open his eyes or stop. He began to groan quietly. I wriggled out of his grasp and crossed the hall to sleep in Annie Jean's vacant bed. I was still awake and feeling like I had violated my mother's place in the home when I heard her come in and go to her room.

I didn't have any way to decline Clifton's nightly invitations to sleep in their bed. I couldn't tell him what he had done, because I was sure that it was an accident, and probably my fault. He continued to do it, sometimes rolling over on top of me and pinning my miniscule frame under his considerable weight. Once, I woke up and ran to the bathroom to wash a slimy white snot-like substance off the corner of my mouth and cheek before retreating to Annie Jean's bed. That frightened me, though I didn't know why. Soon after that, I woke to find my underwear on the floor, and Clifton rubbing himself on me again. Just then, my mother came in, undressed, and climbed into the bed. When they began to have sex, I ran out of the room with my underpants in my hand.

I was confused about all of it. I remember feeling very relieved when Willie came home. Clifton still managed to take "naps" on the weekends, when no one else was home, but he left me alone most of the time. Meanwhile, my grades plummeted and I was in constant trouble at school. When summer came, Annie Jean and Willie left again. I lived through another round of baffling behavior from Clifton and my mother, before I headed off to fourth grade.

My third and fourth grade teacher was a vile woman who hated children, Mrs. Wood. She was a friend of Billy Boy Nunn, and she seemed to single me out on a regular basis for paddling and other punishment. I could count on one hand the number of times I was allowed to join my friends at recess. I didn't bother to hide my contempt for her, because I was a child—children don't learn diplomacy before honesty. I dreaded school, thanks to her.

Once, during the year, Clifton told me that I was too old to take baths any longer. I was nine, and I should be taking showers. He informed me that he was going to show me how to take a shower, and I was to strip and go with him immediately. I obeyed, and the only thing I learned was that the water stung my eyes if I faced the water, and Clifton spent a lot of time washing his penis.

Pretty sure that something was wrong about that, I took advantage of my rare recess privileges to ask my friend Tracy about it. I told her what had happened, and asked her if she thought that was strange.

"Naw," she said, kicking pig feces and farm dirt off of her right sneaker, "My dad does that with me, sometimes."

She was so matter-of-fact, that I resigned myself to let it go.

Clifton continued with the occasional transgression, which always picked up in frequency during the summer. My grades and interest in school continued to dissolve. I knew my father wanted me to live with him, but I didn't think it would ever happen. The social workers had come to the house and tripped over the bags of beer cans in the living room, but left without me in tow. After an incident with Clifton, wherein he drank two bottles of Maker's Mark and sat blocking the front door with a shotgun over his naked lap, threatening us, a social worker came to my school.

His named was Dennis Kitchell. He was a piebald mouse of a man. What hair he did have was orange and wispy. Dennis asked me, a ten year old, if I felt that my life was in danger at home.

"You mean, do I think I will open the door when I go home today and somebody will kill me?"

The principal, Mr. Cherry, dropped his head in frustration, and possibly to hide a smirk in response to my question. When Dennis replied that yes, that was exactly what he meant, Mr. Cherry snapped a look of disbelief at him.

"Well, no." I had to be honest. I thought my family would kill me much more slowly than that.

That ended my father's custody bid.

I had to go to Dr. French's office—seeing as how he was the only doctor in town—because I had been getting sick quite often at that time. I had ringworm on my arm and some kind of blisters on my tongue. I didn't like Dr. French because he was rough when he gave me shots, and he was responsible for the bad allergic reaction I'd had to penicillin when I was younger.

The doctor said that I was anemic, and undernourished. He gave my mother some vitamins for the blisters on my tongue, and a cream for the ringworm. I hated the vitamins, but I took one every day before I left for school. I spit half of it in the gully, every day.

On a nice autumn day, I got into a fight on the playground with a boy that I had a crush on since the first grade. He suckered me, and sent me careening backward down a hill. In an attempt to catch myself with my favored hand—the left one—I broke my wrist. The hand flopped against my forearm like that of a marionette with a broken string.

My mother had to leave work in Cairo to fetch me, and left me in the emergency room of the hospital while she went back to work. I remember Mr. Cherry calling her, and showing me how to make a sling out of a magazine until she got there. She played mother of the year when she arrived. She acted so concerned in front of other people.

The cast they gave me went from my big knuckles to the middle of my forearm. I could still wiggle my fingers and thumb, and subponate or pronate my palm. However, after several weeks, the doctor told me that I would be deformed if I didn't get a new cast (like the girl in the house by the funeral home) because my wrist wasn't healing properly. I had to be anesthetized while my bones were re-broken and reset. They put me in a cast that extended from my shoulder to the tips of my fingers. I did not react very well to the anesthesia, and spent a couple of days in a wheelchair.

That winter, Annie Jean ran away from home. Nobody seemed terribly concerned, nor did they care very much when she returned. She painted over all of her windowpanes with red paint in protest. Willie had discovered debate class, and was participating in impromptu speeches, which I got to enjoy as he practiced.

Clifton disappeared for a long time, after that. Mother said he was in the hospital, and I heard her telling Willie and Annie Jean that something was wrong with his liver, but they weren't sure what. I thought he was going to die, and I couldn't have been happier. We were all gathered in the living room, and I was playing with a doll at my mother's feet, when I said so.

"I'm glad Clifton's gone," I said without looking up, "He's mean and he does stuff to me."

"What kind of stuff?" Mother asked.

"Stuff, like sex stuff," I said. "He made me take a shower with him."

My mother laughed. "I told him to!"

I can only imagine the look on my face as I stared at her.

"I know what he did to you, because I told him to. And he's not gone; he'll be back in another few days."

I wonder if ten is too young to have lost one's will to live. I made myself as scarce as possible when Clifton came home, though I doubt he noticed.

Marcy and my dad were asking questions about home, but I was afraid to tell them anything. I didn't want to be taken away from Willie. My mother be damned, though I believe in the ugly reality of Stockholm syndrome—I wanted to stay close to my abuser. I told them nothing.

In mid-January, I was taking advantage of a snow day to spend some time with a friend of mine, Paula Goaten. Paula lived on the other side of the railroad tracks, on the road south of my subdivision. On the way to her house, I had to cross a wooden bridge that reminded me of a chainsaw slasher movie—it gave me the creeps, but it beat hanging out at home. We played in the snow, forming a snowman out of the wet snow as best we could. I was about to put the head on when Willie came panting up to us.

"You gotta come home, right now. You're going to court," Willie had his hands on his knees and struggled to slow the breath that was curling in wild clouds around his face. "Looks like your dad's taking you."

I wish I could say that I walked home with a heavy heart, or something dramatic. I didn't, though. I just walked home and put on a dress with my snow boots, and got in the car with Mother for the two-minute trip to the courthouse, in the center of Wickliffe. I saw my dad and Marcy, but I was afraid to go to them, with my mother right there. I waited in an office while they entered the courtroom.

When they came out, my dad looked happy. I went home with Mother and she told me to get my clothes together because I was going to live with my dad. I struggled to hide my joy as I stuffed my several-year-old outfits into paper bags. When I moved on to my prized possessions—my toys, my spelling bee trophy, and the porcelain doll that I got from JoAnne—Mother stopped me. She told me to leave them, so I could play with them when I visited. It saddened me to do so, because I knew that I would never return, once I left. My father knocked on the door to collect me, and started putting bags in the back of Marcy's car.

    My mother informed me that he had not won custody. The state had taken me away for neglect, based on my health problems and reports from unknown people. My dad just got me because there was no one else who wanted me. I could hear Willie crying in his room. I wasn't sure if it was because I was leaving, or because he wasn't.

Chapter Five: Adding Injury to Injury to Injury

When the subject of the month-long summer visitation came up, I protested. I didn't want to go, and I didn't want to tell them why. One night, during dinner, I saw a story about a girl my age being molested by her uncle. The house looked similar to that of a girl named Christy that I had known since kindergarten. Shaken, I lost my appetite. I had to tell someone, so I told Marcy.

I don't think she believed me, really. She asked me a lot of questions, grilling me to see if I really had first-hand sexual knowledge. She made me describe the look of semen. It made me very uncomfortable. I suppose I was expecting some sympathy. Once I had convinced her sufficiently, she told me not to worry. She would take care of it.

The world seemed to lose cohesion after that. I had to tell, tell, and re-tell the story of what happened. I told a pair of female counselors, and suffered the humiliation of showing them what had happened using anatomically correct dolls. At my age, I knew all of the scientifically acceptable nomenclature. They wanted me to use the dolls.

"You can do whatever you like to that Clifton doll, Ronnie. It's okay," the brunette offered.

"I think I'll just set it right there. I'm not going to throw it or anything." I responded.

"Why not? Are you mad at Clifton?" the blonde counselor asked.

"Yeah, I hate him. But this," I lifted the little cloth man and shook it, "is just a fucking doll."

Thankfully, my less gracious behavior was viewed as a side effect of abuse.

I told the whole story to the counselors, the sheriff, and the gynecologist who examined me. By the time I got to Terry Johnson, the state attorney who would be prosecuting the case, it was rote. He outlined everything by date and time. We would be going into court in September, and I would testify. It would all be over soon, he assured me.

Once my stepfather was charged with sodomy and child abuse, and my mother was charged with complicity in those offenses, we began to receive death threats. Good southern justice, I supposed. They were indicted promptly.

My father began to carry a loaded revolver with him, not for defense, he told me, but so he could kill Clifton if he happened upon him while he was out and about. My father was understandably angry, but I had no idea how angry he was. In response to the threats, we had to tighten up security at home, adding procedures for my safety and that of little Brandon, in case someone came to the door. The police were alerted, and in response to their "shoot them first, then call us" attitude, loaded handguns were stowed throughout the house. Marcy showed me how to shoot. I could no longer leave the house without an escort.

Even though I had only been attending the new elementary school for a couple of months, I was making friends quickly. I impressed the teacher enough to prompt her to send me to the gifted student program for testing. My IQ qualified me for placement in an advanced group. I was proud of myself, and pleased with the attention. Marcy seemed pleased, as well.

In early March, I heard that Annie Jean had filed reciprocal charges of sexual abuse against my father. He denied them categorically, saying that they were just trying to take attention away from my case. I couldn't understand why they would do that to my dad. It seemed like they could stand to spend a little more time working on their defense, and less time trying to ruin my father's nursing career.

Then, the little house in Wickliffe that had been my home for ten years burned to the ground, taking all of the prized possessions of my early childhood with it. I cried for my loss, at first—though, I knew I would happily have avoided that place forever. Marcy snapped at me, angrily, reminding me that my father had lost more than toys or clothes when the house burned down. He had been paying the house payment for that place all along, and the ownership was his.

I was worried about things that only annoyed Marcy: was the elderly Phillips couple hurt? Was Joey hurt? She sometimes hid under the house and slept there. Marcy spit "no" at me and gripped the steering wheel severely, prompting me to sit in silence for the remainder of the drive to the Wickliffe courthouse, where she had some papers to sign. We crossed the street and took a seat at the counter in Wickliffe's only diner for lunch. I picked at my grilled cheese sandwich thoughtfully, wondering how the house looked when it was engulfed in flames in the middle of the night. We were only a mile away, and Marcy wanted to drive over there after lunch to look at the charred corpse of the house that was the impetus for my creation.

As we approached the gravel driveway, I asked Marcy how it could happen. The house was made of bricks, not wood. She said it might have been an electrical fire, and since no one was home, most of the house was destroyed before anyone called the fire department. No one was home.

I wasn't prepared for what we found at the end of the driveway. The roof was gone completely, having been obliterated by the fire, and the efforts to fight it. Its evidence lay scattered across the lawn. The brick walls were crumbled and heaped around the foundation as if the child that had been constructing the home had been called away to lunch. The word that came to mind repeatedly was "small." The entire house was reduced to a single room; it was a tiny black square on a patch of green. I wanted to wander through the rubble and look for any precious reminder of my past, but Marcy said it was too dangerous. A child should never have to benchmark her maturation with losses like these.

That night, I sat on the back porch with my dad while he drank his after-work beer. I told him that I was worried about Joey, but he comforted me by reasoning that Joey would have run away from the fire, instinctively. My dad comforted me by just being there.

Marcy talked to her parents, gossiping about the fire as if I could not hear her, though I sat in the same room. Watching television did not rob me of my hearing, although it seemed to render me invisible. She told them that the police and the FBI were investigating the house fire. They had ruled it arson, and were checking out all of the people connected to the house. So far, they thought it might be one of Annie Jean's boyfriends, Tommy. I didn't say anything, but I couldn't imagine why Annie Jean's boyfriend would burn down my old house.

On March 26, I went to school just as I usually did. I was nearing the end of my fifth grade year, and was enjoying a normal school experience, in spite of all of the madness at home. I came home in high spirits, after a full day of joking with my friends and singing in the choir. I scarcely noticed that my father's car was missing from the driveway.

No worries or fears plagued me as I walked along the brick walkway to the front door of the red A-frame house that I shared with my father and stepmother, Marcy, and my little brother Brandon. He would be turning three in about two months, or a month after my eleventh birthday. I was quiet as I entered the house, in case Brandon was napping. I had learned to keep quiet when I was near the house, because the baby slept in the room on the ground floor, and his window was next to the porch. In order to keep him cool, the window was left slightly open at all times. From that room, you could hear a car passing on the street. I knew, because it used to be my room—before they sold my bed to make room for the crib. It had become Brandon's room, but I got to sleep in there on a folding piece of foam that changed into an unstable chair during the day.

I noticed that the bedroom door was closed, so Brandon was asleep. I carried my bag into the kitchen to set it down on a chair until I could put it away. I found Marcy waiting for me, sitting at the side chair. She motioned for me to sit down.

"Well," she began quietly. She was holding a folded piece of notebook paper in front of her. "Your father is gone. He left with his friend Johnny, and they are on their way to Utah right now. He had to leave because of you, and your sister, and all the trouble you caused him."

I had never seen her so hateful. She was always less nice when my dad wasn't looking, but never so mean. She was still talking.

"And this little piece of paper," she waved the paper in her hand, "is a power of attorney. Your dad signed this today, and now you belong to me. You are going to get through this court appearance, and we will join him afterward."

"Ok," I agreed, because I was still thinking we were on the same team, with the same goal. She corrected that belief.

"You shut your filthy fucking mouth, unless I ask you a question. You are a filthy animal, and you make me sick. You don't know how to behave. You are a piece of trash just like your whore mother. From now on, you will do what I say. You can start by washing those dishes." She motioned over her shoulder toward the sink.

I rose quietly, and approached the sink, which was overflowing with food-caked plates and silverware, and burned pots and pans.

"And you better keep it quiet," she added as she padded off to the couch. "God help you if you wake up my baby."

I remember the first beating that I got from Marcy almost as clearly as the last. The ones that came between seem to blend, with highlights, like a sports reel on the news. The reason I was being beaten was not always clear or predictable for me, so I developed an ever-vigilant state of terror that became part of my everyday life.

The first time, I had scraped my spoon against the bowl while I was eating canned pasta. I was too surprised to protest when Marcy charged in from the living room and grabbed the back of my hair, dragging me from the table. She was scooping up fistfuls of pasta and smearing them into my face, grinding the heel of her palm into my nose and mouth. All the while, she was shouting a nearly unintelligible stream of curses. She slapped at my face and body until I curled into a defensive ball on the floor, crying in fear and pain. She ordered me to clean up the mess I made, and I did so promptly.

I received similar attacks for eating my favorite food first from my plate, rather than all items evenly. For borrowing a quarter to use the payphone to call for a ride home from a school activity because she forgot to get me (*"We are not a charity case!"*), I got a lump on my head. I got a similar beating for taking a cookie that was offered to me by my friend's mom (*"We are not a charity case!"*). I was never sure what would trigger her wrath, and as a result, I was afraid to do anything without her permission.

She reigned over every aspect of my life. If I developed a blemish, she would pick at it until my whole face was covered with scars and scabs. Once, she told me I had bad breath, and wrapped her hand around my throat and filled my mouth with water and medicated soap that she had on prescription from her dermatologist (her skin was less than perfect).

I was late to get teeth as a baby, and didn't lose all of my baby teeth until the eighth grade. When I knew Marcy, I still had many to lose—one of them, a canine on the left side, showed signs of crowding the permanent tooth through the side of my gum. Marcy spent hours every day, pulling on the tooth—which was not loose, in the least—with a length of string. I remember thanking her through a mouthful of blood when she finally ripped it out of my mouth. I was so relieved.

If I bit my nails—and that was a tough habit for me, I was to be punished with a switching. Switching, for those fortunate enough not to have experienced it, is a punishment in which one's legs are rapidly whipped using a long green stick from a tree until blood welts are raised.

When we were preparing to drive out to Reidland to visit Marcy's parents, the clothing and hygiene inspection revealed that I had been biting my nails. She seemed almost pleased.

"You know what I have to do, now. Go get a switch off the tree."

I began to cry, and like the child that I was, searched the tree for the least painful branch. She burst out the door, complaining that I took too long and selected a long whip-like growth that tore a thin, curled patch of bark as she peeled it from the trunk. She deftly bent over and whipped the stick back and forth across my shins until small beads of blood rose randomly from my knees to my ankles. I was worried about wearing the pink shorts I had on, but was ordered to do so because they and the matching shirt were a gift from Marcy's mother. We hurried to the car, now late because of my disobedience.

When Marcy backed across the gravel driveway, a rattling can reminded us that two full bags of trash had been waiting behind the car. They had not made it into the trunk. Since it was my fault that she forgot, Marcy made my lie on my back and crawl under the car, picking out dirty diapers and torn plastic that had been wound around the axle. I hoped that she would run over me and end it. Maybe then, my dad would have shot her.

I kept monitoring my bloody shins on the way to Reidland, hoping that the swelling would be gone before anyone noticed. I assumed that if Marcy didn't want to be a charity case, she would have definite problems with being known as a child beater. Yet, when her mother asked me what happened to my legs, I just gaped and looked from her to Marcy for some back up. I was too smart a kid to think that I could say I fell down the stairs. I thought Marcy must have been suffering a lapse of memory of apocalyptic proportions, when she offered me no help. She was baffled as to how I managed to do that, and expressed realistic concern. The subject was changed quickly enough and it was forgotten.

At the end of our visit, I said my goodbyes and rounded the side of the house to climb into the waiting car. It smelled like the freshly washed and folded laundry that sat on the seat between Marcy and me. Brandon lolled in the car seat behind us, worn out from a day of coddling. Marcy turned to me, and I wide-eyed, watched her face as it crumpled into a mask of barely bridled rage.

"What was that? Huh? You want to make me look bad in front of my mother?" She emphasized the second syllable of "mother" by reaching across the car and slapping me savagely. The upward arc of the blow struck the underside of my nose forcefully, the momentum causing jets of blood to come gushing out. She grabbed a towel, and thrust it in my face, which I employed quickly to prevent ruining my clothes.

"You owe me twelve bucks for that towel."

As we drove away, I wondered if I would get that much for my birthday from Grandma Schiller.

My father drove all the way across the country, and stopped to take some photos along the way. He sent them, with a letter. I got to see a few of the pictures, but I didn't really know how things were going. It looked as though my dad had been living in grungy motel. He was waiting for us to come, after the trial, to get a real place.

Marcy monitored my letters to my dad and grandma. If they didn't sound happy enough, I had to rewrite them. When my father called, she stood over me while I spoke to him to make certain that I didn't mention the way I really felt. She controlled everything.

Everyone at school thought I was doing great. I was impeccably neat, and driven to do well. I participated in choir, 4H, and every intramural sport that Marcy wanted me to. I immersed myself in books, relying on school as my only escape.

When the summer came, I counted down the days until the trial. Marcy had altered her daily schedule so that she would sleep in until noon or later, and left me to take care of Brandon. He would wake me by throwing a bottle full of sour milk from the night before, and became apt at striking me in the face. He called me "Ronnie-mama." I would feed him breakfast, and watch Sesame Street at a low volume or play quiet games with him until the afternoon. Frequently, he would back into a corner and defecate himself in defiance against potty training efforts. Then, he would call for Marcy until she rose, no matter what I did. The anxiety of that routine—trying to be quiet, and trying to care for a small child with no experience—had much to do with my later decision to be voluntarily sterilized.

In early September, I discovered several blocks of paraffin wax in the laundry room. I asked

Marcy if I could make candles with them. Of late, I had been completing craft projects to keep me out of trouble. I had been learning to sew under her direction, and created several pieces of fine doll clothing, which Marcy gave away. She gladly permitted me to make candles, since we had all of the materials there. The only thing missing was the paper milk carton to use as a mold. I substituted a hydrogen peroxide bottle, which had first been cut in half with our new sewing scissors.

When the time came to pull the candles out of their molds, I went to the kitchen and endeavored to do so. It was nighttime, and the single bulb over the sink lighted the kitchen. The wax was stuck fast inside the brown plastic bottle, so I started to cut it away with the sharp scissors I found on the counter. I was holding the blades open, and forcing them through the bottle, around the wax, in a circle, when they slipped up beyond the mouth of the opening and snapped shut. My left thumb was inside the closing blades.

"Oh, my thumb!" I didn't really feel it, and I couldn't see the damage in the dark. I made a ring of my right index finger and thumb, and gripped the base of the injured finger, not daring to look at it. I walked into the living room where Marcy was watching television, hoping for help with a bandage. I told her what I had done. I was not crying.

She rinsed the cut with cold water as I held my thumb over the sink, and very calmly told me to stay right where I was.

"Don't touch it, and don't look at it. I'll be right back," she started to back away. "You're going to need a few stitches."

I began to bawl as soon as I heard the word "stitches." I had never had stitches, and I was terrified. I felt very weak, like my legs were made of some untrustworthy compound. I leaned over the edge of the sink and caught a glimpse of my thumb, which was a foreign thing to me at once. A V-shaped flap dangled by half of the nail, which was also cut. The top half of my thumb looked like the hood of a coat. I cried all the way to the emergency room. She took me to the hospital where my father used to work.

Thanks to my clumsiness, I spent several weeks with a bandage over my thumb, and I began my sixth grade year writing right-handed, once again. The trial had to be delayed, because my appearance had to be perfect. Yes, it was a miracle that I would be able to keep the appendage; regardless, the trial had to wait until I got the stitches out. We were aiming for the end of October.

Marcy took advantage of the injury in her own cruel way. As the violence continued, I began to fantasize about picking up the handgun in the kitchen and shooting her in bed as she slept. Then, I would think of my baby brother, and I knew I couldn't do it. I turned the hatred in on myself.

One morning, while Marcy slept, I left Brandon watching Big Bird. I lifted the gun from the shelf in the kitchen where it was hidden behind a pewter tray. I felt the heft of it in my hand, and lifted the barrel to the side of my head, to feel it. The safety was on, but I didn't really care.

"You know," Marcy's voice came up coolly behind me, "if you're going to do that, you should really put it in your mouth."

I was shaking when I returned the gun to the shelf. I was pretty sure, after that, that I hated her.

CHAPTER SIX: TRIAL AND ERRORS

Marcy had worked the sort of miracles with my psyche in the six months that I spent alone with her, that would make the CIA blush. I was fully indoctrinated by the end of October, when we made our appearance in court.

My tomboyish look was not sweet enough for the prosecutor, so Marcy applied her skills at creating a more presentable facsimile of me. I climbed into her faded blue Grand Prix wearing a brand new dress; it was gray with tiny flowers all over it, and had ruffles of the same material at the cuffs and the hem, which fell just below my knees. There was lace trim and a maroon velvet ribbon tied in a permanent bow at the center of the collar. I hated it. I felt like some sort of Little House on the Prairie nightgown-clad fraud. The white tights and buckle shoes were no more comforting.

To make matters worse, she fixed my hair for me, as well. My fine bangs were parted in the middle and feathered back into ridiculously girly wings on either side of my face. I was much more accustomed to baseball caps and ponytails, and sat stiffly in the car, trying not to move my head too much.

We parked next to the courthouse, and began climbing the steps that led to the main entrance. So much had happened while I was losing the fight for my self-esteem versus Marcy. The small town that was my former home had been scandalized by the news of my accusations. I had been characterized as a creative liar and a disobedient child. The prosecutor warned us that the courtroom would be open for observers, and I should expect to see a few people I knew in there. He also mentioned that the judge in our case would be familiar. It was Bill Shannen, my mother's attorney from the divorce proceedings and custody fights with my father. He had been promoted to the other side of the bench.

When I asked my dad if that was a bad thing, he said not to worry. I guessed the only way to cultivate a real dislike for my mother was to know her, personally—and to let her humiliate you with her behavior in front of your colleagues. He said Bill Shannen had every reason to be fair. The jury would help with that, no matter what.

The process of finding an impartial jury was complicated, due to the disproportion between the diminutive size of the town and the demonstrative size of the scandal. Members were called from neighboring townships, and distant rural areas, in addition to the few people in Wickliffe who had not already made up their minds. An error in jury selection was corrected narrowly before the start date. As attorney Terry Johnson was reading the list of jurors to Marcy, I recognized the name of Clifton's cousin Patty on the list. She snowed them, having made no mention of her relationship. We weren't certain whether the expensive and slickly reputed attorney that my mother had hired from Paducah had done that intentionally, or if he, too, had been tricked. It didn't matter, once I pointed it out, because she was gone.

We rounded the corner, and made our way to the big front steps. I surveyed the lawn of the courthouse with the sad realization that I wouldn't see it again after that week. I could pick out the spot where the cotton candy cart would be parked for the Harvest Festival and the big sheet where kids dropped over the cane pole to "fish" for a prize. I had been a child of the town—without supervision, almost literally—and the trial would sever those ties forever.

Marcy and I trudged up the stairs to the courtroom foyer, where Mr. Johnson, the state prosecutor, waited for us.

"How are you doing, kiddo?" The big attorney looked like the Maytag Man to me. He opened the door for us without waiting for my answer.

We filed in and took our place at the table on the right of the bench, which was set at an angle, so that our backs faced the door. There were rows of wooden chairs behind us. The left side of the bench belonged to the defendants, who were waiting. All of them were staring at us—at me. A rush of fidgety silence and halting breath rose like an ill wind as we took our seats. The gallery on their side was half-full; ours was barren save for a few reporters.

I fought the urge to stare back, taking scanning glances of the crowd that sat in the gallery behind my mother, stepfather, and their attorney. Many familiar faces stared back at me: Billy Boy, Mrs. Wood, Annie Jean and Willie, and Brother Wells, the man who had been my minister for three years. I felt very small.

The judge came in and took his place at the head of the room. Bill Shannen was a wide man, and the shapeless robes transformed his pale, round face into a floating orb in the dimly lit room. The jury filed in and took their seats in the box across from us. Mother, the great manipulator, gave them all a friendly smile, and batted her eyelashes in slow succession. The thick mascara-caked lashes nearly made an audible click-click as they fanned over her white-outlined eyes in a "poor little me" expression. She was not aging well, and I was glad for every person who had told me that I looked like my father.

The judge began to speak, and some talk passed between all of the tables, but I was in a vacuum, imploding upon myself under the pressure of so many hateful glares. I was shaking, and a little bit sick. All of the words spoken sounded like nonsense to me. Marcy leaned over and listened to Mr. Johnson, then leaned over and tugged at my sleeve, startling me.

"*Whooshoooshoooshooosh* cross...legs," she said. "While you are up there. Don't forget."

At least, that is what I heard. One of the first lessons I learned is that you do **not** ask Marcy to repeat herself—or any other adult, for that matter—in her presence. I applied all of my lessons at that moment, and came up with an interpretation: *Don't forget to cross your legs while you are up there, because you are wearing a dress, and you need to be lady-like.* That must have been what she meant, I decided, because I had a tendency to sit with my knees sprawled, and that would embarrass everyone, wouldn't it?

I was called to the stand, which was actually a chair on a pedestal directly in front of the judge. Johnson came up and gave me a brief pep talk to comfort me, though, like his greeting in the hallway, I sensed that it lacked earnestness. I supposed he was showing the jurors that I was just a kid, and needed comforting, in case that was not obvious to them. In hindsight, I believe that the case would have been easier for him if I had been less intelligent and spoke baby talk.

He asked me the questions pertaining to my mother's involvement that we'd gone over in his office. The story was laid out with care, detailing all of the events, and emphasizing the criminal moments. As I answered all of his questions, I crossed and uncrossed my legs uncomfortably. Then, the slick big city lawyer came to cross-examine me. I really didn't like him. He made me uncomfortable, and I struggled to remember to keep my legs crossed when I talked to him.

"Did you ever know your mother to take drugs, Ronnie?"

I wasn't sure what the angle was on that one. Of course, she took drugs! All those parties and the roach in the ashtray verified that. However, I wasn't sure what he was trying to prove, and I didn't want her getting away with anything.

"Yeah, I remember the time she ODed." I added a little extra volume at the end, "If that's what you mean." I guess I could play innocent, too—or dumb.

When he asked me about my mother's mothering habits, he seemed to have hung himself. I verified that she had indeed cooked dinner for me: once. No, I didn't think she even knew how to use our vacuum cleaner. He asked me questions that didn't really make sense to me. I fidgeted and shifted in the hard wooden chair.

When he was finished, Judge Shannen called a recess for lunch. We had two hours to get some food before the trial continued with my testimony about Clifton. Marcy and I walked out to the car, and left the parking lot headed up the street. All of the bad people would be getting lunch at the diner in Wickliffe, so we would head over to La Center or Barlow to eat. Yet, there we were, pulling into the first parking lot entrance on the right, on the other side of the Baptist church that was next to the courthouse. Wickliffe: it may have been the county seat of government, but it was home to five churches—which was better than one church for every hundred citizens.

Marcy parked the car, took a deep breath, and slapped me broadly across my right cheek. She proceeded to yell at me for crossing my legs on the witness stand. She had told me not to. She said I looked too casual and nonchalant. She used the word "nonchalant" many times.

She also told me that the only reason Clifton didn't stick his penis inside me and hurt me worse was because he was a drunk and he couldn't get it hard enough. She told me he was probably a repressed homosexual, and experimented on little kids because they wouldn't tell. She said I could thank my mother for this happening, because she probably knew it all along.

"And if your mother gets acquitted," she finally yelled, "you can live the rest of your life with no one to blame but yourself. It will be your fault, because you didn't listen to me."

We went to lunch, and when we returned, I was ready to give the best testimony known to man. I was going to cry, or Marcy would give me a reason to.

I sat at the table and observed the testimony from Marcy—the ever wonderful, caring stepmother—and then from Annie Jean. Her testimony was more damaging to Mother than mine was—she told about her responsibilities in the house, and how she acted as the caregiver since she was a child, herself. She affected an attitude of disinterest and general disgust toward the whole proceeding.

Mrs. Wood testified at the beginning of the second day, and painted a shining portrait of her admiration for me for the court. She thought I was a brilliant, creative child—though given to telling "stories" occasionally. I was a pleasure to have as a student. She used the manure she called testimony under oath to present me as a calculating child who liked to tell lies to her, the loving teacher. I nearly chewed a hole into the side of my mouth, listening to her lies.

Willie took the stand that day, as well. The experience was horrible for me. He testified about how close we were, and how we did everything together. He told the court that I had never told him about the abuse. As he described the way I used to come running up the street to meet him each day, he began to cry. He turned to me, and shouted in a half-sob, half-whine that coaxed me to recoil in shame, my face contorted in instant tears.

"Why did you do this to us?" He was beginning to hyperventilate. "Why? Why? Why!"

His was the last testimony I witnessed. After his outburst, Judge Shannen stopped everything and had Marcy escort me out of the room. I spent the remainder of the trial in an office down the hall, watching the pigeons strut along the concrete ledge outside the window. I was left in the care of an old friend.

"Do you remember me, Ronnie?" The man looked worn and aged, but I knew his face. I nodded.

"Dennis Kitchell," I glanced at the smooth shine of his balding head before returning my attention to the lush courthouse lawn. The super social worker looked as though he had humbled in the few years that had passed since our meeting in Mr. Cherry's office.

"Ronnie," he paused, waiting for me to acknowledge him. "Why didn't you tell me?"

I felt sorry for him, because I knew my father "had his ass" after the state awarded my custody to him for neglect. I heard the word "reprimand" and "suspension" in my dad's conversation with Marcy. Still, I knew he could have saved me, but he failed me.

Turning my focus back to the view of nature below, I replied without feeling.

"Why didn't you ask?"

He retreated to his desk, remaining silent henceforth.

Marcy reported the progress of the trial to me as we rode home each afternoon. My mother played innocent, stating that not only was she not involved; there was nothing in which to be involved. Marcy said she was waiting for my mother to burst into song at any moment, favoring us with a rousing rendition of Tammy Wynette's "Stand by Your Man." Every question her attorney asked was turned into an opportunity for Mother to slander my father. Eventually, this led Judge Shannen to threaten a contempt charge against her.

"Missus Nunn, if I have to remind you one more time that Mr. Schiller is not the one on trial, here," Bill Shannen boomed, face reddening, "You are going to spend some time in my jail. Take care, now. Proceed."

I was glad I didn't have to sit there and swallow my anger in the face of all those lies. I just wanted it to end. I knew that when it was all over, I'd be leaving Kentucky to join my dad in Utah. I'd be in a new place, with new people. I would get to start over in a town where no one had heard of my slutty sister, and nobody would think Ronnie was a funny name for a girl.

On the last day, I sat in the second floor office, ignoring Dennis Kitchell, and scrawling pictures of birds and trees on a legal pad until shortly after noon. Marcy and Attorney Johnson came in and sat in the vinyl covered office chairs, looking exhausted, as though they'd been fist fighting to settle the matter, rather than talking. Marcy's navy and white Swiss dot-style dress showed dark circles of sweat beneath her arms.

Deliberations were under way. There was no way for us to tell how long the jurors would take to discuss and decide the fate of Mother and Clifton. We decided to get lunch at the diner across the street, but neither of us was very hungry. I had a glass of lemonade, but spent more time examining the sunny liquid than drinking it. I could feel the momentous nature of the day, but I was not tense. I wanted it all to be over, and I was sure they would both go to the darkest prison forever because I was just a kid—you can't hurt a kid like that and get away with it.

There was still an inch or two of lemonade remaining in my glass when Attorney Johnson leaned in the doorway of the diner and motioned to Marcy for us to come.

"That was fast," she remarked to him.

"Is that good?" I didn't like her tone. Her response that she wasn't sure did little to comfort me.

We hurried back into the courthouse, and filed into our chairs at the table, as before. It seemed as though the crowd had grown in the gallery. The jury foreman stood and gave a folded paper to the bailiff, who passed the same to the judge. He looked it over before he spoke, ordering the defendants to rise.

"Before I read the verdicts, I will remind you that this is a court of law, and you are expected to keep your comments to yourself," he directed this to the crowd across from us. As he finished speaking, I noticed that three sheriff's deputies had stepped up to surround our table, and a fourth stood between our table and theirs.

"As to the defendant, Eugenia Faye Nunn," Judge Shannen cited the various charges of complicity and abuse of a minor, which meant nothing more than gibberish to me, "we, members of the jury find the defendant not guilty."

Not guilty? There was a collective sigh of relief across the room. My stomach sank as I saw my mother smirking satisfactorily at me. I knew it was my fault, just as Marcy said. The judge was still reading.

"...on all of the above charges, we find the defendant, Clifton Curtis Nunn, guilty."

An instant explosion of noise erupted from the gallery and the table where Clifton and my mother sat. I heard wails of torment, and shouts of disapproval and protest. I saw Billy Boy's arms flailing around the shoulders of the deputy who restrained him. My preacher rose to his feet and proclaimed that I was possessed by the devil, to which Billy Boy agreed vehemently. I saw Annie Jean crying. All of these events happened simultaneously, as the sheriff's men were pushing me down, creating a human shield around Marcy and me. They were pushing us out the door and down the back stairs when I heard a loud bang, and some scuffle behind us. I heard Willie's tearful voice calling, "Ronnie! Ronnieeeee!" It faded behind the heavy door as we ran out to Marcy's car that waited for us.

We didn't speak or stop until we reached Paducah. Marcy used a payphone in the parking lot of a fast food restaurant to call my father and let him know what happened. As she made a second call, I noticed the police car behind us. I wondered how long he'd stay—and how long I was going to need him to.

The next morning, I was surprised to find myself boarding a plane to Utah—my first flight. I didn't even get to say goodbye to all my beloved classmates. I flew under an alias: my middle name and a new last name. I considered switching to my middle name after I moved, but it didn't feel right: too girly.

Seeing my dad again was like crossing over into the imaginary world you'd read about in a picture book. He didn't seem real, only Marcy's world was real. I remained vigilant and cautious, as I would for years hence—but my father made me much happier.

As we left the airport, my new homeland repulsed me. I had just left the sunny beginnings of a crisp Kentucky autumn, but I arrived to a dark, gray, lifeless landscape. There was snow on the ground in filthy piles, and the sparsely growing trees were little more than black sticks. On the horizon, where there should have been a familiar fringe of dollops of oaks, maples, and poplars, there was a great, craggy point of muddy slate-colored mountain. It seemed to break into the sky and clench it in a jagged fist. It was far too cold for late October.

I softened upon viewing the road that led to Stansbury Park, the small community that would be my home, with its great millpond and poplar-lined road that led into the area. I was told that the empty fields to the north were alfalfa farms, and beyond those were the southern shores of the Great Salt Lake.

Chapter Seven: Take the Girl Out of Nature

Until Marcy and Brandon were ready to join us in Utah, my father continued to live in the deplorable kitchenette apartment that had been his home since May. I stayed with a friend of his, an anesthesiologist with too much money for his own good, a wife who barely spoke to him, and two spoiled kids. The girl was nearly my age, but her interests were childish and feminine. They boy was too young to play with, and was only interested in playing the drum set he they kept on the back patio for him. They did, however, have an Apple II desktop system.

The best part of the summer that I spent with Marcy was that she did everything she could to get me out of her hair during the day. I played every sport she could get me into, despite the fact that I was awkward, uncoordinated, and gangly—and I ran and threw a ball "like a girl." I am assuming by her criticism that Marcy did something otherwise.

I attended vacation bible school at the Hope Missionary Baptist Church. There, I was told that: 1) I was going to go to Hell because I wore blue jeans to vacation bible school the first day, instead of a modest dress; 2) I was going to go to Hell anyway, because I had not been baptized by the time I was 8; 3) being in Hell would be like an eternity of suffering in the worst way imaginable—eternity, by the way, was defined as the time it would take to fill the room completely full of spit-wads. The sad part is that the rocket scientist who came up with that analogy was entrusted with the souls of children.

I found happiness at the summer computer camp: a day camp for kids to learn the ways of the personal computer. I found my niche, there, learning BASIC commands and plotting little colored squares to create pictures. I won a free sundae at the Dairy Queen for my depiction of a pink rose on a blue background. I liked the computer because it was predictable and manageable. I told it what to do, and it did what I told it to without fail. The experience formed a significant part of my personality.

While I spent my time at home with the anesthesiologist's family buried in computer programming adventures, school forced me to be somewhat sociable. Stansbury Park Elementary School followed a new protocol, in that they separated the students into skill levels for all courses, dividing the disciplines amongst several teachers. I had a homeroom teacher, Mr. Smith, a science teacher, Ms. Wilson, and all of the kids got together for Ms. Hadley's art class. I spent most of my time with Mr. Smith, because they didn't have course materials to match my skill level. He managed my curriculum personally. Since they didn't have reading coursework for anything above ninth grade level, we discussed the books I read in my spare time, and added them as an assignment: mostly, The Lord of the Rings trilogy by Tolkien or the collected short stories by Ray Bradbury. For mathematics, I completed exercises from a pre-Algebra text, combined with fun computer programming exercises. The whole class got to learn about computers, once a week, but I spent hands-on time with the donated Apple II-e daily. My final project for math was a 10-page code printout of a "Choose-Your-Own" story adventure featuring characters from Tolkien's books, written in Apple BASIC.

The boys in class continued to mock me and tease me because of my drawling Kentucky accent. They would turn around one moment and ask me how to spell a word for their paper, then moments later call me "hillbilly" and laugh at me. After a couple weeks of that abuse, I asked to be moved away from the farmer's sons. Wisely, or perhaps coincidentally, Mr. Smith had me sit next to Sheila Shastead, (pronounced shyaah-stid) a curly-locked blonde girl from Wisconsin. She was perky and friendly without being cloying, and soon our conversations had bent my tongue in such a way that the drawl was completely lost. After a month of living in Utah, I spoke like the people on the news, and my relatives in Chicago didn't sound so funny anymore.

Marcy, Brandon, and Marcy's parents were another story entirely. To me, they sounded ridiculous, while I sounded "like a Yankee" to them. I suppose the Pilgrims felt similarly, when they found their children speaking Dutch. Marcy ordered me to stop using the new accent, but I could not. Trying to put the drawl back on my speech was like trying to fit little baby slippers back on my feet.

Through that conversation, I learned that Marcy and Brandon would be joining us before Christmas. I was thrilled to have my little brother back, and excited to be able to live with my father again. Even though he was always working, having him in the same house was better than having him live in some motel outside of town. I tried not to think about Marcy, and hoped that she would behave, with my dad watching.

We moved into a condo on the millpond side of the community, next door to Mr. Smith and his family—though, I rarely saw them. The interior had the all-white plaster walls, gold shag carpet, and slightly cat-like odor indicative of a rental community. The minuscule kitchen adjoined a laundry room with a half bathroom—something I had never heard of—but the living room and dining room had vaulted ceilings, and the bedrooms were quite long, if not very wide. I shared a room with Brandon, but slept in a bed instead of on the folding foam. The window in our room faced eastward, with a clear view of the dreary spike of the Oquirrh Mountains. Since we were too far from the school, I began riding the bus to school, rather than walking. The changes were mostly positive ones.

My father had to work on Christmas day, so we woke up at four in the morning to open our gifts. I was used to him having to work so often, and he was new to the hospital, so wasn't able to arrange for the holidays off—those with seniority got to spend the day with family. I hadn't the energy to be concerned with the holiday, anyway. It was hard for me to fake a smile for daddy, with Marcy back to her old tricks the minute his car left the driveway.

School in Utah was not like the schools I attended in Kentucky. I quickly learned that the kids were divided into distinct social classes and groups, and that I didn't belong to any of them. I was as nice as I could be to everyone, but it made no difference because my family was not as wealthy or as Mormon as the other kids were. My hair and clothes were all wrong. I never sought out solitude, thought it often found me. My friends were fewer than usual, but I did my best to get along with everyone.

Some of the kids in my grade stood out above the others, as being better known, more popular, or more talented. Talent, in Utah, was not based on intellect, from my observation. It was measured by the amount of time a girl had spent in a local dance troupe, or how often a boy had sung with the choir on Sunday. Using that scale, Katie was very popular. Tanya, her best friend, was talented, and so was Tanya's boyfriend, Brian. The three were inseparable, and powerful by sixth grade standards. I knew of them, and they knew me. It never went the other way.

Marcy always pushed me to be more social than I cared to be. She wanted me out (of the house) with my friends, and somehow arranged for me to have friends when she could do so. When I made friends of my own, I was almost guaranteed success if I asked for permission for a sleepover. That's how I got to spend the night over at Lisa Berry's place in the end of January. I liked Lisa because she was smart in science class, and at the same level as me in math class. When I talked to her, I didn't have to explain everything. It was more fun, that way.

Lisa wanted to go ice-skating on the frozen millpond that night, so I took along my Lake Placid Flyers—that had not touched ice for over a year. I'd never been skating on an actual pond, but I wouldn't admit that I was a little scared. When it came time to go, Lisa's mother said she was too tired to drive us there. Despite Lisa's wheedling, we were stuck inside for the night, playing board games.

When I got home the next day, I heard my father telling Marcy about the rescue workers that had been treated for frostbite the night before. Some girl had fallen through the ice on the west side of the millpond while skating. They were still out there, chopping up the pond with boats, looking for the body.

"Why didn't they dive in and save her?" I butted in with a heavy "it's not fair" tone.

"It's too cold," my father dismissed me neatly. "The guy diving in would have died too, and it's not worth it."

"But a lady died!" I persisted.

"She shouldn't have been out there, in the first place. And," he continued, "It wasn't a lady, it was a girl and her friend. They didn't have their parents out there, or anything."

By Monday, the story was confirmed, and rumor had given it hideous detail. Katie and Tanya had gone skating Friday night behind Katie's shoreline home. Tanya was a bulkier, taller girl than Katie was, and had skated out farther than she should have. When she fell in, Katie—star lifeguard at the summer public pool—tried desperately to pull her out. She threw a scarf and tried to tow her out by sprawling on the ice with the tips of her skates dug in and pulling. Eventually—some speculated that it was the cold, others, the acceptance of impending heaven—Tanya just gave up, pushed back, and sunk under the surrounding ice. When the rescue team arrived in response to the neighbor's reports of a girl's screams, they found Katie sitting on the ice, in shock, still gripping her scarf on one end, while the other end dangled half-frozen in the hole.

I had never dealt with death. I understood death; I knew that all of us would eventually die and that it was a part of life. I took a tour of the funeral parlor next to my school in the third grade, and saw the coffins where they put the people who died. The people who lived upstairs in the grand building showed us how they made ears and noses out of wax, so the dead people would look nice for their families. We read *A Taste of Blackberries* and *Bridge to Terabithia* in class: stories about children dying suddenly. Still, I thought my father's lack of sympathy was cold-hearted and cruel. The entire school was in mourning, and was closed the day of Tanya's funeral. I attended, because I had nowhere else to go.

The scene was staggering: so many children crying, and adults comforting one another. Tanya's body lay in white coffin, with white satin inside. She looked gray and unnatural with orange-tinged makeup all over her face. Her lips were purple. She was wearing a rose-colored chiffon dress with ruffles that was far livelier than she was. When Brian leaned in to kiss her, I shuddered and looked away. Tanya's dance troupe sang "My Favorite Things" for her, and I have not been able to hear it, since, without thinking of a dead 12-year-old girl.

My heart was broken for Katie. The survivor has to carry all of the pain of death; I knew this, even then. I knew what it was like to live choked with guilt. When I saw her at Tanya's funeral, I could tell—even from five rows back—that the flame had been snuffed from her eyes.

More rumors at school followed Katie's progress. She was listless, and haunted. Some of the kids said that Katie was going to psychiatrist, but it wasn't really helping. I thought of Mother.

One day, I was in the girl's restroom, and I came out of the stall to find Katie standing in front of the mirror. She was practicing a smile; a grisly visage with forced cheer that reminded me of the excessively cosmetically treated Tanya in the rose-colored dress. I wasn't sure she even noticed me, behind her, because she jumped a little when I asked her if she was all right. She turned around and hugged me, withering in my arms. She cried there for a few minutes, and I let her. Rumors reported that she moved to Boston right after that, and her parents sold the beautiful house on the millpond shore.

CHAPTER EIGHT: OUT OF THE FRYING PAN

My twelfth birthday is probably my most memorable.

I was never sure what started the festivities that night. I remember my father coming home from work in the early evening. He was wearing his white lab coat, and he asked me if I wanted to go bowling. Of course, I wanted to go bowling; I was twelve. I would have done just about anything to get out the house. I had grown bored with watching Brandon's cartoons. I was more than ready to escape Marcy. However, there was some kind of problem: Marcy didn't want to go bowling, or she didn't want to take Brandon to a bowling alley. Some sort of disagreement came up; wherein she had the unbelievable gall to not only tell me how I was going to spend my birthday, but how my father should spend it with me. She began to nag him about all manner of things, while I retreated to my bedroom across the hall and stood in the middle of the floor, letting the panic seep in. I hated confrontation, especially when Marcy was angry, because it usually led to something unpleasant for me.

Just as I started to feel the peak of nausea, their bedroom door burst open and I saw Marcy charging toward me. Without the slightest pause or glance over her shoulder at my father—who followed her at a fairly brisk pace of his own—she reared back and slapped me across the face with enough force to send me careening into the dresser.

Considering that my over five foot high frame was only carrying around seventy pounds at the time, it didn't take much. I swear, she actually smiled when she saw me fall. She had performed a similar stunt when I was eight or nine, with a bit more flourish.

That had been a visiting weekend, and I was laying in my bed, trying to coax myself into sleep. I didn't like sleeping in the dark room, and my psyche still considered it a strange place. The A-frame's hardwood floors transmitted every change in pressure, as well as every sound, with audible clarity. I heard a brewing disturbance in the bedroom above mine. Loud whispers became shouts, and then Brandon began to cry. Stomping footsteps crossed the room, came hailing down the stairs, and to my doorway. Marcy grabbed my arm, near my armpit, and dragged me as I struggled to gain footing, up the stairs. She jerked me to my feet at the foot of the bed where my dad sat, consoling Brandon, and smacked me hard across the face. I had no idea what was happening.

"You hurt me, I hurt you," she told him proudly, "And I know what hurts you."

My father and I left the house that night, and spent the night in a motel. He took me to a buffet and told me that wouldn't happen again, and please don't tell my mother. On my birthday, though, he handled things differently.

The smile had just begun to break across Marcy's face when my father's big strides caught up with hers. I pulled myself up the front of the dresser, making use of the drawer pulls, in time to see my father grasp a fistful of Marcy's orange hair. He lifted her off the ground and tossed her into the opposite wall effortlessly. I wanted to cheer, but I stood dumbly watching. I wanted him to punch, kick, and strangle her as she had done to me, but he just grabbed me and we went down to his car and drove away. Violence is not something that can be subtracted: positive violence will not cancel out negative violence. It wouldn't make me feel better, and no single punishment would heal a year of verbal and emotional abuse.

We left, and drove to the truck stop at the junction in the interstate. We sat in the diner and talked about things that didn't really matter, while I ate the best-tasting grilled ham and cheese sandwich I had ever had. When my dad left to use the payphone, I hoped that he wasn't calling Marcy to make up with her. I wanted to continue to be free.

"Ok, Ronnie," he took a deep breath as he sat back in the booth. I braced myself for the worst. "We're going to go meet my girlfriend, okay? She's got kids your age, and we can go stay with them, okay?"

I smiled through a mouthful of ham and cheese, and nodded happily. Anything had to be better than Marcy.

That night, we took the long route to get to Faith's apartment. She and the kids lived 56 miles north, on the eastern side of the then-flooded Great Salt Lake. The apartment was messy, with piles of clothes and dirty dishes, and I loved it. No psychotic control freak would live in a place like that.

Faith was a nice, doe-eyed woman with a heavy, curved body, enormous breasts, and actual blonde hair. She had that dropped-lid look reminiscent of Miss Piggy from the Muppet Show. She was so warm and kind to me, and I was happy be there. After a brief introductory chat, she and my father retreated to the bedroom, leaving me alone with the kids.

The three kids that were to become my new stepsiblings were slovenly miscreants, aged seven to twelve. The youngest was a girl named Jessica: terminally cute and petite, with long, fine blonde hair that had never been cut. She was giddy about having someone new in the house, as was the middle child, Keri.

I later found out that Keri was taking regular beatings from the oldest child, so she was probably hoping for an ally. Keri was the ugly duckling of the bunch: her ears protruded at a hilarious angle, and her nose was flattened grotesquely from using it to brace a fall she had taken from a crib when she was an infant. Her bottom teeth were brown and smashed together because of a tetracycline dosage given to her at an inappropriately early age, while the top ones flared out in unnatural directions and overlapped each other horribly. She was good-natured, and sweet, which made up for some of her gangly oddness.

The boy, Mark, was one month older than I was. He was pudgy, and seemed to act as if he knew everything about everything. He was protective of the girls, and offered to protect me, too. He smoked Marlboro Reds and wore camouflage pants. He stayed up all night, talking to me about what happened to me in the few years before we met: him, with his camouflage pants, torn t-shirt and blond hair, and me in navy slacks, penny loafers, matching navy and white cardigan, and meticulously parted and clasped brown hair. I could tell, already, that none of these kids was terribly bright.

We did our best to be like a family. My father continued to work at the hospital near Stansbury Park, and drove me to and from the Stansbury Park Elementary School each day so I could finish the year. It made me sad to think that I would be moving yet again, and I wouldn't attend junior high school with any of the kids I'd gotten to know.

The last day of school was full of the usual goofing off, so I took an instant camera and a pad of paper to create my own yearbook, of sorts. I shot photos of all my friends and favorite teachers using Faith's camera with the cracked lens. All of the shots have a gray wedge-shaped marking in the corner. I had the students sign the notepad, leaving their impression for posterity. Most of them were silly. I also carried a white t-shirt, which everyone signed with black or blue markers—for the more creative kids. It ended up getting wet, and the well wishes blurred into one dark smear.

That evening, there was a gathering in the gym—a dance, according to the flyers—for the sixth grade students. My father insisted that I take Mark with me, so he could meet my friends and have some fun, as well. I was not thrilled with the idea of keeping Mark busy while I celebrated my last romp with my buddies, but I obeyed in the spirit of brotherhood.

The dance seemed to be going well. Mark caught the eye of a towering blonde named Cassandra, and they were slow-dancing—a humorous sight, considering she held the height advantage by at least a foot and a half—in the middle of the floor, with a few other young couples. I was chatting up some of my friends, and listening to tales of their tour of the gigantic junior high school in Tooele. I didn't even notice Mark and Cassandra, sneaking off the floor into the corner.

Suddenly, Mark approached me, and urged me to take something for him. He wanted me to get rid of it, quickly.

"What?" I didn't bother to hide the disgust on my face as he grabbed my hand and plopped a sandwich baggie full of prescription drugs into the middle of my palm. I stomped into the girls' bathroom and flushed the multi-colored contraband unceremoniously. I was enraged that he would bring such garbage into my school.

So was Cassandra, who found me as I exited the bathroom door. She menaced me, leaning over me and spluttering rage at my "brother" who tried to sell her drugs. Drugs! I assured her that I knew nothing about that behavior, as I had just met him. I apologized, and dragged Mark outside to sit with me silently for the rest of the night. While we waited for my father to arrive, I wondered what ever possessed the boy to bring a baggie full of antibiotics, tanning pills, and vitamin e capsules to an elementary school.

By the end of June, we had found a house for us to share in Layton. Compared to the condo, and the apartment, it was palatial. I got my own room, in the basement next to my parents' room. It was disgustingly feminine, with baby blue paint on three walls and the ceiling, and white wallpaper with tiny blue flowers on the fourth. The carpet and the blinds matched the paint, and big lace curtains edged the window. I didn't mind, though. I got the best room in the house.

That summer, I also got something I had needed since the second grade: eyeglasses. Until I put on my glasses for the first time, I had never realized that a person could see the leaves on a tree, or that there were so many stars in the sky. I had been near-sighted for so long, that I felt like I had never really seen the world at all. I could ride a bike, and jump with it on a ramp. I could read signs on the side of the road. I could suddenly do anything.

However, the choices I made and the responses I exhibited in certain situations were colored by the perception I had of the world because of the way I was treated. I often justified horrible things that happened to me so I wouldn't have to feel bad about them later.

After we moved to Layton, I developed a crush on the 14-year-old boy that lived on the corner. He was blond, loud, and pushy. He was obnoxious in the way that boys can be, and not mentally stable. He tortured the neighbor's cats, set things on fire, and said lewd things to me when I walked past his yard. I thought he was terribly cute. I would write the standard 'I like you, do you like me?' notes and toss them over the fence at him. It only got worse when Mark befriended him. He was ever-present in our home during the summer days, while our parents were away at work.

One such day, we were playing in the house, chasing each other. I ran into my basement bedroom, and he followed me. He pinned me to the wall beneath my window, and began grinding his hips against me. I wriggled loosed and tried to leave the room, still playing chase. The door wouldn't budge, and Mark's giggle on the other side told me why. The panting boy pulled at me, tearing me from the door, and pushed my 70-pound frame to the floor.

As I shouted and cried with pain as he penetrated me, I could see Keri watching through the spaces in the blinds of my window and hear Mark shuffling outside the door, still giggling. It was over quickly.

In order to make myself feel better, I told everyone he was my boyfriend. I allowed repeat performances, and told myself it was consensual.

When I began seventh grade, I had almost every strike against me. I was tall, too thin, and most of my clothes were a few years behind fashion; most of my clothes were more than a few years old. I was still trying to style my own hair, which left it unevenly parted in the middle and pulled back severely with a barrette on either side of my head at wildly mismatched angles. These attributes, combined with the thick glasses, the too-large front teeth that contorted my closed-mouth grin, and the bad skin, made me a prime target of everyone's ridicule. Seventh-graders are the lower class, as it is, but I was one of the worst.

I was called every name but the one my mother gave me. Every ride on the bus was torture. I was shoved, tripped, poked, and pulled. They shot saliva-soaked balls of paper through straws at me, threw paperclips at me, and called me "Peabody." One boy set my hair on fire with a lighter at the bus stop. It took him almost ten years to apologize for that. I took all of this abuse silently for most of the year.

During the winter, I fell in with a group of bad girls from around the block: the Wynn sisters, Erin and Hailey. They were average 1980s ratted-hair rocker girls, from their jeans sewed tight to the skin (which we called "pegged") and black concert t-shirts, to their eye makeup and generic brand cigarettes. Erin—the bruiser—was in the eighth grade, and Hailey—the beauty—was in the ninth. They taught me how to shoplift for them, and how to peg my jeans so they weren't so baggy—not entirely successfully, with my bony shape. I was a sort of pet, along with another eighth grade girl named Stacy. They helped me cover every wall in my room with posters and magazine photos of rock bands that met with their approval.

Stacy pierced my ears with a safety pin and a couple of ice cubes. The ensuing infection was a minor nuisance, compared to the trouble I was in with my parents. Faith did her best to keep me a child as long as possible. To avoid punishment, I took the sisters' advice, and ran away from home. It was a short stay at Stacy's house.

Some of the harassment died down with Erin protecting me. Most of the trouble had originated with her and her friends, in the first place.

The last three months of seventh grade showed the greatest improvement for me. I found a friend in a spunky red-haired girl from my band class—a fellow clarinet player—named Joy. Joy took me under her wing, and showed me how to dress, and to use a curling iron on my hair. She had the benefit of having an older sister and a rarely present mother, which was the perfect combination for sleepovers. Her birthday party fell very near my own birthday, and it was a great night of normal kid stuff for me. I even met my first "real" boyfriend, Brandon, at the party. He was a nerd like me, and very quiet behind his glasses. I wasn't wearing mine, because I had to showcase the lovely eye makeup done by Joy's big sister for me. I remember feeling silly but elated when he gave me a little peck goodbye. We exchanged phone numbers, but kids who went to different schools, as he did, might as well have been on another planet.

I spent nearly every weekend at Joy's house after that. She spent a few at mine, but found Mark to be too creepy for her comfort.

The rock posters came down and the clothes changed to the "new wave" style—though, the craziest thing I did to my hair was part it way over on the right, and sweep the long tresses to the side, sometimes with a small braid in the front. Erin and Hailey badgered me about the new style, but there were far more kids like me than like them.

The reason that it took me half the year to meet Joy was that she was attending Layton's other junior high school until her mother moved them to the new house. I assumed that I had just been wrapped up in myself, but that made sense. There were many kids at her birthday party that I had never seen before. She had been a student of North Layton, but moved to Central Davis. In the middle of the summer, I learned that I would be doing the opposite: North Layton would be the fourth school in three years, for me. I was not pleased with giving up my friends, or with the fact that I would be walking the 1.9 miles to school and back, each day, instead of riding a bus. Utah winters were not kind, and I looked on the impending year with dread.

North Layton Junior High was very similar to Stansbury Park Elementary in its social division. Once again, I was the odd one out. I kept my head low, and made a few friends, but I missed hanging out with Joy. I discovered a few boys, but no one kept me amused for long.

One boy, a ninth grader named Shane Crow, became the object of a strange crush for me. He was sarcastic, and full of snappy comments. He was disrespectful of the band teacher, and made the kids laugh. Though not very attractive, I thought he was the coolest. I began to exchange notes with him, to try and persuade him to pay attention to me.

Shane's first suggestion was that I break up with my steady boy, Eric. The implication was that he would be interested if I were single. Eric was a very nice—albeit effeminate—boy from the semi-popular group. He was so happy and outgoing, and wanted nothing more than to hold my hand as we walked the halls. He was just so sweet, and it hurt me to dump him, but I did it for Shane.

Shane's response was to laugh at me, and I deserved it. I continued exchanging notes with him, every other day, or every day. I was elated when he gave me his phone number. Calling him was a waste, however, because he couldn't be bothered to speak to me. I had no idea how far he was beneath me.

Winter seemed to be darker than usual for me. I felt hated by all those around me, and started throwing strange tantrums at home for ridiculous reasons: one such was over the privilege of wearing makeup. At school, I became the new target of the school bully, Lori Swanson.

Lori Swanson was the six-foot with spike-heeled boots rocker girl who led a gang of black-clad, scary girls who took sheer delight in terrorizing anyone they didn't like. For some reason, Lori hated me. My first encounter with Lori was shortly after Christmas Recess. I returned to school with a new locker partner, Bridget Barnes. She was a tall, gawky girl from my band class—a clarinet player, like me—who had not yet grown into the height that would add so much to her beauty in high school. She agreed to let me share her locker after Christmas because my locker partner Becky, though nice, was hogging the space.

North Layton was a smaller school than Central, and sprawled on a single floor east and west of the main foyer. Long hallways extended in each direction to form a rectangle. I was working my way eastward, down one of these long hallways, when Lori swooped down upon me.

"Hey, Geek!" She was right next to my ear, from nowhere. I was probably just not paying attention, as I had a habit of looking at my feet when I walked anywhere. "You're a fuckin' geek! You hear me, you fuckin' loser nerd!"

I heard her just fine, since she was yelling approximately half an inch from my eardrum. I decided to keep walking, thinking that the faster I left her space, the better she'd feel about me. I didn't make eye contact. Instead, I just tossed my head to the right, thus moving my long hair back over my shoulder. It was a nervous habit.

"You are a fuckin' GEEK!" she shouted, again. People were looking.

"No doubt." I agreed with her, still looking at the floor.

"No doubt," she mocked me with a haughty tone. "You think you are better than me?"

I knew I was dead. I began to stammer and whine.

"I—I just agreed with you! What?" The last part tapered into a slight whine, sounding more like, "whaaaaaa——aaat?" I didn't even care about the people watching after I looked up to see Lori and her army of evil hellcats glaring at me. I swear Kristin Gunter licked her chops.

The ninth grade English teacher appeared at the end of the hall, and Lori began to walk away, telling me she was going to get me later.

For the next two days, I kept a low profile. All of my friends introduced me to the mythology of Lori Swanson. She had lived a lifetime of bullying and mayhem. She was feared by all, and avoided by most students. I was lucky that I had avoided her for as long as I had. Luck only goes so far.

At the beginning of the next week, Lori's gang caught me alone in the girls' locker room after gym class. I was changing out of my gym suit back into my clothes. I never took an outright shower, mostly because of learned modesty issues. Moreover, I didn't want anyone to see how ugly I was. I was grateful for the proximity of clothing that day.

I was trapped in an alcove full of lockers, surrounded by angry-looking girls. Kristin Gunter, the second-in-command, grabbed me and pushed me back into a locker. I shut down, mentally, preparing for a beating. I had no fight in me.

"Can I take the winner," the croaking voice that rose over Kristin's shoulder was that of our Physical Education coach, Ms. Motley. Good old, butch, Ms. Motley. "Or, should we skip that part and go to the principal's office right now?"

We all went to the principal's office, and I didn't have to explain anything to him. He looked as though he'd been bullied in his day. I'm sure I didn't look like I could start a fight with anyone, either. He let me go. Things were quiet, for a time, after that.

By the middle of January, I wasn't sleeping well, and a new interest in the occult was occupying most of my dreams when I did. I still spent nearly every weekend at Joy's house, and she fueled my interests by building Ouija boards and playing with them when we were alone. I had a feeling that something awful was going to happen to me.

My father began talking about moving to Spokane, in passing conversation. I didn't want to move again. I didn't want to give up my friends and start over—especially in a town famous for rain. I missed the sun, as it was, in the middle of another dark Utah winter. I was afraid he meant to do it.

One weeknight in the end of the month, I became hysterical and cried inconsolably over something simple that Mark or Jessica had done. My father tried to settle me down, and when he couldn't, turned to the medicine cabinet for help. He gave me a broken half of a 1mg tablet of Ativan. I slept through the night, and half of the next day. When I woke, he told me that he let me stay home from school. I seemed to need the rest. When he left for work at two o'clock, I was cleaning my room. During the day, I swore that I could hear voices chattering over my thoughts.

CHAPTER NINE: DON'T SAY I GAVE YOU NOTHING

St. Valentine's Day loomed on the horizon like a swollen thundercloud on my adolescent mind. I was single, and still in pursuit of the ever-rapier-witted Shane. I wanted to call someone mine for the romantic holiday, and the occasional depraved groping from the neighbor boy was not going to suffice. I wanted someone to dance with me at the school dance and be smitten.

I was examining every boy in every class, and comparing notes with my friends, trying to determine to whom I should devote my efforts. It was a frivolous pursuit, but I found it more interesting than the English course I had to sit through every day. That woman could scarcely spell her own name, let alone teach English grammar.

Bridget hated Shane. She thought he was ugly and mean. I knew he was some of the first, and plenty of the latter, after what he did to me with poor Eric. Still, I wanted his attention, for some reason. I knew he wasn't dance material, so I shifted my covetous eyelash batting and sighs to a boy in my Spanish class named Brett.

Brett was an unsuspecting thirteen year-old boy: very sweet, introverted, and blissfully unaware of all girls—Miss Ronnie Schiller, included. He had an angelic face, spiked black hair, and an overall neat and attractive appearance. I heard that his birthday was in early December, and my horoscope book said I would be a good match. This is how some thirteen-year-old girls make decisions. The usual recon activities ("I have a friend who thinks you are cute, do you like her?") yielded no good news. ("Ronnie who?")

It was strange that Brett's disinterest in me decimated me. He was a schoolmate of mine until we graduated from high school, and I never had any interest in him, again. I wasn't even attracted to him, later.

The big dance was coming up on Friday, and Valentine's Day was on Saturday. My drive to find someone to belong to had failed. Overall, I felt like a tremendous failure and a reject: "Filthy," as Marcy had put it, and a "fuckin' geek," like Lori Swanson said. Mostly, I was tired of trying to work my way against the current to be normal.

My father was at work on his usual 3:00 PM to 11:00 PM shift at the Davis Hospital, and Faith was working the regular 9 to 5 plus commute, about 45 minutes north of our home. The kids were home alone until six o'clock or so, every day. I closed myself up in my bedroom so I could read, write, or listen to the radio—this was the usual custom. Teens like their privacy, and I was no exception. When Faith knocked on the door and asked me if I wanted to go to the store, I told her I was doing homework. She didn't push the issue, but left Keri under my supervision and took Mark and Jessica with her.

I lay across my blanket, feeling worn. I did not want to go to that dance the next day and stand around in the corner, begging some loser to throw me a pity bone. I decided to call Shane.

He was his usual, calloused self. We talked about Valentine's Day, which he thought was stupid, and about school. When he started insulting me, I joined in. I certainly couldn't argue. He said it was "messed up" that I agree with the worst sort of cuts against me. I told him how I felt. I said I was thinking about killing myself.

"Why don't you?" he offered. Maybe he thought I was bluffing.

"I will," I said, "I'll just go right across the hall to the bathroom and my parents have pills in the cabinet. I'll take them all, and that will be that." I knew, right then, that I could do just that.

"Go ahead," he said. "I dare you."

I told him, fine, nice knowing you, whatever, and hung up. I went into the hall and placed the phone on its cradle as I walked into the bathroom.

I locked the door behind me, and pulled the sample boxes of Ativan out of the cabinet and set them up on the sink. One by one, I opened boxes and bottles, pulling out the contents—one tiny white tablet from each—until there were ten. Since I had forgotten to take a glass with me, I used the cap from the mouthwash bottle. Once I had swallowed all ten, I went back to my bed to think about dying.

I grabbed my bible, and just held it for a while. I hoped that God would understand why I needed to die after all I'd lived through, and forgive me. I didn't feel tired yet, but I knew I would. I decided that I wanted to talk to Joy, so she could remember me happily. I grabbed the dark brown phone and dragged the extra-long cord under my door. It blended nicely with the carpet.

I stretched out on my belly on the bed, with my head near the door, at the foot of the bed, so the cord could reach. I called Joy, and just started shooting the breeze. We talked for a while, but my speech started to slur.

"Are you drunk?" she laughed.

I changed the subject. I knew I didn't have much time. I told her that I found a way to keep my father from making me move to Spokane—in reality that was the last thing on my mind when I swallowed all those pills—and she seemed relieved.

"Oh! You guys aren't going to move?" It occurred to me that she wanted us to stay.

"Well, they might," my speech was considerably slurred, now. "I'm not going anywhere."

"What—hey—what did you do?" Panic touched her voice.

"Oooohh, nnnnothingggg, heeeyyyyyy," I was working hard to get the words out and stay awake. "Yoooooooou arrrrrrre my besssht frennnnn, Joy."

"Ronnie? Ronnie!" She jarred me awake for a moment, "What did you do?" She was almost frantic.

I managed to stammer that I just took some pills and it was okay. I was sleepy. My body felt so heavy on the bed, as if I could just sink into it and cocoon. Then Joy's mother was yelling into my ear.

I told her I took some pills, no big deal, don't worry, and it will be fine. At least, that's what I thought. The unintelligible mutterings that came out were probably just enough for her to make out the word "pills." I'm sure Joy explained the rest.

Then, the darkness came and I was gone.

"Oh, God! Oh, God, Ronnie," I heard a far-away voice, calling my name. It was Faith. The phone was pried from my hand, and I thought I saw of glimpse of Keri in the doorway. Faith was gripping my arm and dragging me to my feet by the bed, but I was made of liquid rubber. I flapped and flopped, and my head lolled around as if my neck had no bones.

"Come on, now. Come on, walk it off, walk it off!" She was trying to make me walk in a circle but every time I tried to plant my foot, the blue carpet would ripple and bend like water. I was bobbing up and down on the surface, but she continued to drag me and repeat her pleas.

I wanted the darkness back.

Suddenly, my dad was there. He helped Faith prop me up in the doorway, and handled me a bottle of salty, thick syrup to drink, which I did obediently. When I opened my eyes again, I saw a large blue octagonal plastic tumbler full of water in my hands.

"Drink up," he ordered, angrily, and I did.

I looked him in the eye, and he pointed to the toilet. I knew he had given me ipecac, an emetic, to make me vomit.

"Just like your mother," he barked viciously. Then, the darkness returned.

I woke for a moment in an elevator. I recognized my father's coworkers over me and I became angry, knowing I had failed. The anger found a comfortable place inside of me—it stayed for a long while.

I woke again, and one of the nurses asked me why I took all those pills. She was so distraught. Some young male doctor was gingerly trying to apply an electrode to my chest around my bra. What a pussy! My inner voice was full of venom. The outer voice was not much better.

"I took all those pills, retard," I enunciated sharply, "because I wanted to die. Duh!" With that summation, I lost consciousness until morning.

My father has told me that I stopped breathing during the night, and had to be revived. Apparently, Faith's efforts to wake me made things worse by increasing the circulation and spreading the drug through my system. I cared about neither fact for many years.

When I next opened my eyes, I saw the pillow end of that old familiar folding blue foam coming at my face. I realized that I was being lowered into it, and glanced around the living room. The sunrise was just breaking over the Wasatch Mountains and poking fingers of light through the nylon drapes. I commented that the rays of light looked like angels on the back of the white couch.

When Faith's hand snapped over her gasping mouth and she began to cry, I sneered into the pillow. Christians are so easy to dupe. I slept away half the day.

I was easily the most hateful human being on Earth when they dragged me to the Davis County Mental Health office. My father narrowly missed warning the counselor not to ask me why I took the pills. I replied as I had to the nurses the night before. I heard him laugh a bit—from either amusement or disdain— when her face puckered up in recoil.

I was still under the influence of a large amount of sedative, and dozed while they discussed my fate. I woke long enough to pile into the van, and then slept all the way to the foothills in East Salt Lake City.

I don't remember being taken to the ward on the fourth floor of the Western Institute of Neuropsychiatry (WIN). I vaguely remember being shown around by a very pregnant nurse that looked just like a health education teacher I once had and liked very much. My parents left me with their goodbyes, and I collapsed on a lovely pink bed to sleep off my high.

I never imagined that I would wake on St. Valentine's Day to find an anonymous valentine card and a chocolate heart on the desk in a room in a mental hospital's adolescent ward. I was quite alert, having slept off the Ativan, and I was more angry than sad. I had failed, and even God hates failures. Right, Marcy?

The place was alive with young patients getting breakfast, and having their blood pressure and temperature taken. Some of them were being weighed. It was a nearly full house.

A counselor with Grave's disease named Tom—simply Tom, no last names in WIN—explained the rules to me. I was locked in, and would only leave if I met certain criteria and completed tasks given to me. The first task, he announced, was to write my story. He handed me a lined memo book. Once I completed the task to attain Level One, I would be given shoes and be allowed to watch television with the other patients. Level Two, as they called it, permitted me to attend school inside the building and exercise in the gym. The Levels progressed all the way to Level Four, which included family visits, weekend passes with family, and outings in the hospital van to see the city with the group and a couple of counselors.

I did as I was told. I was assigned a permanent counselor—a Ken doll-like marathon runner named Heike, who was the ward heartthrob—and a team of doctors, in addition to the regular counselors. My medical doctor, Bruce LeBrecque, was wiry and bald, with round wire-rimmed glasses and a grotesquely protruding Adam's apple. My psychiatrist was a soft, short, mustachioed man named Doug Grey—ironically, he was colorblind and often wore only yellow or blue in addition to brown. Between the two of them, I was bound to find good health, sooner or later.

In mid-March, I was told that Dr. LeBrecque had discovered the illness behind my suicide attempt: bipolar disorder. He explained this to my father, as I listened. His horrible bedside manner included treating me as though I was an infant savant. The disease is hereditary, he said, and sometimes skips a generation. He added that it was didn't usually manifest in one so young, so there might be hope that I could grow out of it, after adolescence. He was going to prescribe lithium carbonate and keep an eye on me.

He scrutinized my dad and asked if there was anyone else in the family with manic-depressive illness.

"Just her mother," he told the doctor with a sheepish grin, "And her mother's mother. That I know of."

"That will do it," LeBrecque glibly replied as he wrote in my chart.

Thanks, Mother.

Part of my rehabilitation was facing people in my past to talk to them about how I felt. I spoke to Joy and apologized for putting her in the position I did. She was my friend, and I didn't mean to hurt her. She was graceful about receiving such a call from the mental ward, but I could tell that things had become strained between us. My experience was changing me.

I placed a call to Marcy, determined to get her to apologize for what she had done to destroy my self-esteem and take the very life out of me. All I need was her admission of wrongdoing. Heike sat next to me as I spoke to her from the dining room phone.

I told her where I was, and how I got there. I told her that I felt that the way she had treated me had affected me negatively, and played a large role in my desire to commit suicide. It was hard for me to say what I needed to because I was still afraid of her. She listened to everything, and waited until I had stopped talking to reply.

"I didn't do anything to you that any good parent wouldn't have done." She sounded as if she actually believed what she was saying.

"But...but...but," I stammered in disbelief. It wasn't supposed to go this way. "You hit me! You slapped my face and punched me, and I was a little kid." Heike tensed beside me.

"You deserved it." She was perfectly calm and sure of herself. I, on the other hand, was frustrated. I handed the phone to Heike in a gesture of complete disgust and disbelief.

The next round did not turn out much better.

This time, I called Shane. I don't know what I expected from him; perhaps, the respect I deserved for having the guts to carry out his dare. I was wasting my time, and that fact was soon painfully evident.

"So," Shane rambled, "do you wear a straight-jacket in there? You guys, like, weave baskets with your feet, and shit like that?"

The day would come when his attitude would improve, but not for a few months more.

I was transformed by the influence of so many other troubled kids around me. For a while, we were like family and I was the baby. Everyone sought to take care of me, and to help me. I was the proverbial ray of light, and I liked it that way. While I was inside there, I never had to clean the house. I couldn't be picked on or teased by the other kids at school. All of the adults were kind, and the boys were enraptured.

We knew about the other's pains and quirks, and judged no one. I suppose that was the opposite of my real family.

Group therapy was an ugly experience. I harbored the anger of having my suicide foiled, and family therapy was a chance for me to inflict my cruelties. I didn't want to leave the safe and blameless hospital ward, and I began making ridiculous demands in our therapy sessions to prevent that from happening.

The family therapist was a warm, fuzzy type of blonde woman. I hated her soft, non-confrontational manner, and the way her nose wiggled up and down like a rabbit's whenever she spoke because her top lip was too short to cover her teeth.

"Ronnie, your parents have said they would like for you to come home." wiggle, wiggle "What would it take for you to go home, Ronnie?"

I leveled my gaze directly at Jessica. Her youthful cuteness and her hair and her spoiled baby talk made me want to retch. She was the antithesis of everything dark and baleful that I had become.

"Kill the little brat," I snarled, "and I will consider it."

Another week passed. The guy in the room next to mine stole a fast kiss before we went to bed one night, then he broke out by setting off the fire alarm. He was still at large when I met Jeff at the day school.

Jeff was an outpatient who attended school at the hospital because his mother didn't think he could handle high school. She would know—she was the head of the board of education for the state.

School in the hospital was easy, on all counts. We attended for three hours, with a fifteen-minute break in the middle. Some curriculum was covered, but most of the study was independent. The transient nature of the student body prohibited structured lessons. We were monitored closely, and expected to stay busy. There was no chatting or touching permitted. Jeff was slick enough to find his way around everything.

I was studying, or pretending to study, some of the lessons my family brought from my teachers. Some of them had included messages of encouragement. Jeff half-turned in his desk and asked for a piece of paper.

I handed him the folder, and he wrote on it, "Hello, I love you. Won't you tell me your name?"

Having recently become a huge fan of The Doors, I recognized the lyric. I gave him credit for a great pickup line.

Jeff was my great love for a year or more, though for no reason I can think of.

We found out that my escaped neighbor had been discovered in the home of a friend. He was housesitting so it took several days for anyone to discover his body, minus the head, in his living room. Well, the head was there, it was just all over the wall. I had a knack for sending men to their graves, or to the military.

As the end of March neared, I began to look forward to getting out. I took a weekend pass with my family and insisted that we drag Jeff along so we could spend the whole drive cuddled together in the back of the family van. When I returned at the end of the weekend, we had new "family" members in the ward.

One of them was a fierce young man named Darryl. He was a skater, and had a rotten attitude—which I loved. We had instant chemistry, and spent many an evening sneaking kisses out of the view of the nurse's station. In that same manner, we shared pieces of nicotine gum.

He told me that he ended up in there after threatening to kill the boy, Gerry, who stole his girlfriend. He cared more about his girlfriend than anything in the world, he told me, and this Gerry guy snaked her away. He was going to get him, someday. I felt sad for him. I was sad to say goodbye in the last weekend of March when I got out of the hospital and returned home. A few of the other patients were released that day, and I exchanged phone numbers with them so we could keep in touch.

When I got home, everything was normal—regrettably so. I missed my friends, and the always-clean surroundings of the ward. I didn't like my family's expectations of me, and I wanted to get out and enjoy my freedom. When I received a phone call from Steve, a seventeen year-old who was in the ward for about a week, I was willing to play along with whatever he planned.

My dad was planning to take us out to a very expensive steakhouse in Salt Lake City. I said I'd love to go, but asked if I could meet some friends at the mall for a couple of hours, first. I hadn't seen anyone for a month. He agreed. At the time, I didn't even think about what an asshole I was.

Steve came by in his white pickup truck, and I climbed in. He had a friend with him, so I was sandwiched in the middle of two attractive, older teenage guys. I had no complaints, even when they started passing around the marijuana pipe in the truck as we sped down the interstate. I had very little regard for dangers to my life, at the time. I smoked with them as we drove all the way to Sandy city: about 20 miles south of Salt Lake City, to a party in Steve's neighborhood.

When we arrived at the party, I was greeted jovially by all of the guests. I was treated like one of the group. One of the girls said I was "so cute." I was introduced to another girl with my name, though she spelled hers "R-A-N-I." Aside from that, she was unremarkable, so our conversation was awkwardly brief. By the time I made it to the kitchen, I could no longer remember the names of the people I met by the door. This was compounded by the fact that I was not wearing my glasses, so I couldn't see any of their faces clearly, and that I had been smoking marijuana for hours.

There were several cases of Rainier Beer in the kitchen, so I popped open a tall can and tried to drink it down. One of the girls in attendance, noticing my involuntary grimace, came over and showed me a trick that she had employed to make the nasty beer go down a little easier: she was cutting it with grape soda. Grateful for the advice, I followed her lead, and plowed through the better part of a 12-pack that night.

Somewhere near my second beer, the crowd greeted a new arrival to the party raucously. I heard my name called, and when I looked up, I noticed that it was my nicotine gum-chewing friend, Darryl. We were as old lovers united, and headed off to the bedroom to alleviate some of the pent-up sexual tension. Unfortunately, no matter how many times we tried, we were always foiled by some interruption. Finally, a slobbering drunk girl came in and collapsed next to the bed. I surrendered when she began orchestrating hand motions choreographed to Pink Floyd's "The Wall," which was blasting through the speakers in every room of the small house. Darryl and I talked for a while about the fact that he was out on a weekend pass, and had to go back to the hospital on Monday. He then left for home.

I returned to my binge drinking, which had been interrupted. I sat quietly on a couch, while everyone around me talked and made noise. I was getting to be quite intoxicated, when Steve's friend from the truck came and sat next to me. He was tall, and nearly wrapped his entire self around me like a wall when he sat down. He asked me what happened to Darryl, and in my stupor, I told him. I said we just gave up, and he left.

"I can't believe he would just give up on you," he said, touching my chin, "You're just so pretty."

Sucker.

He kissed me, and kept kissing me. Suddenly, we were right there on the couch in the middle of the room, and he had his arms around me and we were making out. I could hear the reaction of the "nice" girls in the room around us.

"Hey, isn't that the girl who was just screwing Darryl?"

"Skank!"

I turned my head and frowned shamefully in the general direction of their comments. They didn't understand. Darryl didn't want me. My partner in crime grabbed my hand, and led me out the front door. We passed someone who was on all fours, vomiting, as we staggered around the corner to Steve's house. It was cold and dark outside.

We lay down in Steve's bed and had drunken sex. When it was over, there was a lot of kissing and cuddling that I found unnecessary, but sweet. Though I was sure he had told me his name in the truck, I couldn't remember it. I asked him again, as we dressed.

"Gerry," he said, laughing. "Don't you remember?"

"Too much weed," I managed. Oh, fuck. Darryl was going to be pissed.

We moved our private party back to Gerry's house, sneaking into his bedroom. It was nearly three o'clock in the morning when I phoned Jeff to tell him what I had done. I spoke to him while I sat straddling Gerry—both of us clothed, though he was obviously aroused—as Gerry lay on his bed. This epitomizes my relationship with Jeff, in all its strange glory.

Jeff managed to tell me that my parents were looking for me, and that they had sent the police out after me, just before his mother took over the phone. She didn't sound groggy or sleepy, and I soon found out that she had been awake when I called, though not because of me. She had been preparing to deliver Jeff's twin sister, Jennie, to the hospital in a few hours. It's a small world. She would be along to gather me up and take me in, as well. I agreed to wait for her.

When we returned to WIN, Jennie and I got to be roommates.

Jennie, and most of the other kids in the hospital, came from wealthy, conservative families. It seemed to me that they ended up in a lockdown because their parents had neither the time, nor the understanding to handle their rebellion. The kids hated wealth because they had money, but nothing else. One girl was in there because she set aflame the GUCCI watch she was given for Christmas, along with the fully decorated tree. The same girl used to wear paper cereal bowls on her head, and call them yarmulkes. Jennie used to give away her possessions, and cared very little for what she had. I distinctly remember watching her pry her braces—just the brackets, there were no wires—off of her teeth. I wished that my parents would spend money on improving my appearance. I had trouble understanding the problems of the wealthy. They seemed sad but petty.

The girl at the far end of the ward had been in the same room for nearly eight months. She was a ballerina, and a very good one, named Heather. She was also a double eating disorder (anorexia and bulimia) victim who nearly killed herself to stay thin as a young teen. She was a beautiful, subdued, and graceful girl, though she bore a slight mustache due to the anorexia. She took a matronly role where the other eating disorder patients were concerned because she understood them. I did not, on the other hand. Many of the patients thought that I was anorexic when they met me, because I was grossly underweight when I began my stay, despite my voracious appetite. Heather was concerned for me, at first, as well. I liked her.

When she overheard me telling Jennie about my party weekend with Darryl, I was surprised to find her so upset about it. I assured her, it was not a big deal. I meant, "it" was no big deal. She was not amused, and walked away with visible anger. Darryl's return to the ward and the remainder of his stay filled in the blanks for me. I surmised that after

I left, Darryl and Heather had begun to cultivate a "true love" relationship full of honoring and cherishing. I had accidentally exposed Darryl's duplicity, and I was sure he never expected to see me again. He yelled at me for ruining his relationship with her, because I was clearly the one at fault. I felt a lot better about having sex with his nemesis after that.

By the time I left, everyone seemed relieved to see that the medication had piled enough weight on my bones to bring me from just-over 70 pounds to around 100. I was not comfortable carrying that much weight, and would not be for years to come.

Doctor Grey continued to talk me through all of the drama and trauma that my life had created around me. He decided to put me through some testing, just to confirm or dismiss potential problems I had in dealing with other people. The most elaborate was the IQ test. He wouldn't tell me the exact MENSA-ranged result, but he gave my father a hint: it was about twice that of my father. No wonder I hated my English teacher; she was stupid. Doctor Grey said there were some studies that found a correlation between IQ and bipolar disorder, so he wasn't terribly surprised.

My attitude of disdain developed a new twist, after that.

As my fourteenth birthday approached, I became eager to return home—for real, this time. I wanted my life back. My demands in group therapy became more reasonable. I had one wish, and I got it on record, in front of the whole family.

My father always ended his workday with a six-pack of beer. I had been aware of the practice since I was six or seven, and it never bothered me.

After the days of Marcy, though, after Brandon was taken away from him, he drank more and more until it seemed like he was always drunk when he wasn't working. He was verbally abusive. He hit Mark and Faith, and me, once. He was destructive to himself, and damaging to everyone else. Even though he singled me out to be spared from his worst abuse, his doing so divided me from the other kids in the family and made it difficult for me to get along with them. We were never a "mom-and-dad-and-kids" kind of family; we were a "your-mom-and-my-dad-and-me-and-you-guys" sort of family.

So, before I was ready to go home, I made my dad promise to stop drinking. Everyone was there to witness the promise, which I compromised from "no drinking" to "no getting drunk." I believed in moderation. No one told me that his degree of alcoholism was an all-or-nothing situation in which moderation was an unrealistic option. The sunny-blonde therapist negotiated the offer: As long as my father didn't get drunk again, I would stop trying to hurt myself. This deal included my newly developed penchant for cutting small holes into my wrists.

We agreed, and I was ready to go home. Two weeks later, his end of the deal fell apart in Jackson Hole, Wyoming. We were celebrating my birthday in a restaurant and he was in one of his obnoxiously loud moods. He shouted, rather than spoke, and the content was inappropriate for mixed company. I asked him quietly to calm down, but he just got worse. Faith and Mark provided the support to my observation that he was embarrassingly drunk, despite his denial.

"Fine," I said with pure lucidity. "All bets are off."

I never wanted to admit how much it hurt me that my father would choose to get drunk, knowing that his sobriety was the only thing keeping me from cutting my wrists, or trying to kill myself again. I didn't understand, but I didn't act on it—at least, not for a while.

I finished the eighth grade on my own terms, vaguely aware that I was being a pain in the ass and taking advantage of the pitiful, conflicted administration. I managed to switch English courses, citing extreme stress and personal conflict with my teacher. I knew it would be more effective than simply stating that I hated her.

To most of the student body, I was a late-arriving new student. None of them had really noticed me before. I returned with a new hairdo, darker makeup, and a new mode of dress that was edgy and leaned toward a punk-skater hybrid. I looked more like the kids from the Salt Lake City high schools, or the kids from the hospital. I also had pressured my parents into getting me contact lenses to replace the thick glasses that I repeatedly mangled and smashed to avoid wearing them. Even though I sported a new look, I harbored an old bitterness. No matter how I appeared on the outside, I was ugly on the inside. That, no matter what your mother tells you, is what attracts other teens in droves.

There was some mythology created to explain my disappearance in the month I was gone. Some said that I had died, while others told a gruesome tale of my failed attempt to shoot myself in the head that left me disfigured. I had reached a sort of cult status amongst the disenchanted. The—extremely ridiculous by my adult standards—graphic, gothic poetry that I wrote as an outlet won me several unlikely fans, as it was passed around the school and photocopied repeatedly: including Erin Wynn and her metal band boyfriend, and my former tormentor, Lori Swanson who suddenly regarded me with a degree of respect. I wrote piles of rhyming poetry, detailing the soul-deep darkness and the bloodlust that consumed me. It was pathetic, and effective.

I enjoyed being maleficent. When a spunky little cheerleader in my English class—I knew her, you can bet, her name was Emily and she was popular—leaned over to greet me, I thrilled at the chance to take a swipe at her.

"Hi!" She smiled with all her perfect teeth, "Are you new here?"

I eyed her over with a look of distaste before settling on eye contact, and replied, "No. I've been here all year. You've just never seen fit to acknowledge me." With as much ennui in my voice as I could express, I added, "Go away."

She didn't deserve it, but it felt so good.

When summer came, I tried to return to normal. I was not like other kids my age, and I could feel that. It was as if I had been dipped in an evil solution that soaked into the center of me, leaving the outside unmarred. I had knowledge that the other kids didn't, and it permanently changed my perception of the world.

My father persuaded Mark to join Civil Air Patrol, to get some discipline and direction. I visited a meeting or two, myself, and acquired something unexpected: a boyfriend. Faith was nervous because Ben was old enough to drive, and she made me take Keri with us whenever we went out. In truth, Keri was protecting him more than she protected me. He was terribly mousy and the only thing I knew about being with a boy required the removal of clothing.

When Ben left for a student tour of Europe, he made me promise to stay out of trouble while he was gone and not to self-harm. I'm not certain that I ever meant to keep the promise when I made it, or I didn't think I'd be around to feel bad about it.

My parents decided to buy a puppy, so my father and I went to the pet store and picked one we liked. When he came home that evening, he brought the puppy with him—but not the one that I wanted. Faith and the girls picked a prissy lap dog and my father complied. He made a wager with the puppy's life against my own. The terms were that the little dog would be put to death if I tried to harm myself again. I hated that stupid-happy cocker spaniel.

When I overdosed that summer, I did it out of spite. My parents were rationing my lithium, keeping the bottle hidden in their room, so I wouldn't have access to it. I resented them hiding it from me, and I intended to give them a lesson in my ingenuity. The biggest insult was that they told Keri where the bottle was so she could administer my afternoon dose—that imbecile. As soon as they left for work, I ran into their room and found the hidden bottle easily. I filled an empty peach schnapps mini-bottle with capsules and put everything back where it had been. The mini-bottle was returned to the top of my dresser, where it had been displayed as a novelty for untold ages. The dark brown plastic concealed the contents.

Throughout the day, I avoided food, and intermittently swallowed handfuls of pills from the bottle. I took my scheduled doses as they were given to me, never letting on what I was doing. By dinnertime, I had taken over 30 capsules at 300 mg each: about a week of medication. I felt nothing, though, until I ate hot dogs for dinner with the rest of the family.

I retreated to my room to take the last of the pills from the mini-bottle. They were sticky and soaked with schnapps, and a few of them tore apart when I tried to convey them from the bottle to my mouth. Lithium tastes like rusted, dirty nickels, and that, combined with the schnapps, was too much for my stomach. I vomited into my waste paper basket. Disappointed, I trudged outside to clean it up, thinking my plan had been foiled.

I had to walk through the den, passing between Faith and her children sitting on the sofa and the television. When Faith questioned where I was going and then why, I told her the truth. I continued outside without looking back, and used the hose to clean the wastebasket. By the time I returned, she had put everything together in her head. She promptly put me in the car and drove to the Emergency Room. Despite my protests as to the futility of the treatment, they made me drink ipecac. I knew there was nothing in my stomach, since the contents were so recently dumped out of my garbage can. The nurse told me, as I was violently heaving syrup and water, that I was lucky I was a nurse's kid. She said normally, they would have pumped my stomach as a punishment for a stupid stunt like that. There is nothing pleasant about being treated for overdose when one is completely aware.

I served overnight stay in the ICU, in the care of our family friends and my dad, himself. The doctor charged with my care was annoyed, but informed my father that he felt that I was worth saving. By late morning, he determined that the risk of coma had been eliminated, and I was ready to go home. My first words to my father were loaded.

"So, did you kill that stupid dog yet?" I was as contrary as can be.

"No," my father sighed and fiddled with my IV, "I think we'll keep the dog."

"God, you can't keep any of your promises, can you?" I learned to hurt people by watching him. He should have been proud.

When my parents took me to my usual outpatient appointment with Doctor Grey, they surprised me in the WIN parking lot by pulling a suitcase out the back of the van. Talk about ingenuity. They checked me in, and I was back in the lockdown within a few minutes.

It was a tantrum-filled couple of weeks in the adolescent ward. I made no friends, and was nobody's darling. When Doctor Grey put me on permanent Level One, I screamed and called him a prick. I told him his kid—he'd recently fathered a baby boy—would probably hate him because he was such a pompous asshole. I felt bad when I noticed that I'd made him cry, but I continued to rage. I ran down the hall, screaming profanities at the injustice of it all, and climbed into the space in the corner behind the headboard of my bed. I buried my face in my pillow and refused to come out.

A counselor name Will who had been a friend in the past, happened to be working. With his Mississippi-native accent and easy-going manner, he reminded me of my brother, Willie. I bet Willie went by Will, as an adult. I would have. Will came in my room, and started asking, and then ordering me to get out, which I ignored. As if the bed were a toy, he yanked it abruptly away from me, startling me a little. Will made it clear that if I wanted to suffocate myself with that goddamned pillow—goddamned!— he was not going to stop me: he'd just wait for me to pass out and lock me in the seclusion room so I could wake up in bed restraints.

Suffocation was never my intent, and I told him so.

"Well, kid," he softened a little. "This is not a country club, and you are killing your parents, being in here. And I like you, girl, and I don't want to see you in here, either."

I cried several months of anger all over Will's powder-blue Guayabera shirt.

I missed my father's birthday, the Independence Day celebration, and Ben's return from Europe. Ben forgave me, but was soon gone, having joined the Army.

Ninth grade was my most normal year. I invested my time in studying, and making real friends.

CHAPTER TEN: ARRESTED DEVELOPMENT

I could never decide what I really wanted. In high school, and college, I never had a clear-cut answer as to what I wanted to be when I grew up. I still don't know. I didn't have a family or a church, or a limitation to my own talents to narrow the path for me. I believed that I could do just about anything, if I took the time to learn, so I settled on nothing.

It was pretty much the same situation when it came to relationships. I never knew what I wanted, so I just sort of went along with whatever happened to fall in my lap. I wasn't saving myself for Jesus, or marriage. I wasn't holding out for Prince Charming. I thought that the right one would come along and everything would magically fall into place, but I had no model for what that would look like.

For several years, I thought that the right one was a friend of mine, Andrew. We became friends one day in ninth grade when I sat down next to him at lunch. He was sitting on a concrete bench in the foyer, being introverted. At the time, I was obnoxiously extroverted, and I wanted to draw him out. I viewed it as a challenge. I sat next to him and made him talk to me. He was drawing a picture of a train, and he was quite talented. I noticed that he was left-handed, like me.

I had seen him before. He was in band class, briefly. We had picked on him, then. He was also in my journalism class. When we tested for our staff positions, he scored one point below me. That made me managing editor, and he was my assistant editor. I knew he was smart.

I continued to talk to him, whenever I saw him. At first, it was a matter of meeting the challenge to unleash the introvert. By the end of the year, I had grown fond of him. I considered him a great friend and I thought it would always be that way.

High school brought the populations of Central Davis and North Layton junior high schools back together. High school threw me back into the mix with a lot of people I hadn't seen since I was twelve years old and still very forgettable. I saw Joy again, and was disappointed to find that she had become dark and gothic, and was in the habit of taking LSD. I supposed that I was lucky to pass through that phase and back out before high school came along.

I was sharing hallways with another classmate from Central Davis—a boy I had a huge crush on, Neil. He was in the brass section of band class, but never knew I was there. Somehow, I always sighed when I passed his yearbook photo while I reminisced about my time at Central. He had not changed much, but he seemed to like the way I turned out. We hooked up early in the year, and I thought it was a dream, come true—so like a teen movie. Nevertheless, he was a 15 year-old boy, with no money, and didn't consider taking me to the Homecoming Dance. I kept thinking he would ask.

That's why, when Andrew asked me, I said I couldn't go. I was completely shocked that he asked me. I thought to myself, if he and I went on a date, it would ruin everything. I didn't have enough faith in myself to be able to maintain the friendship. I didn't know what a relationship was really about—I just knew sex, and that had ruined a perfect relationship with the rosy-cheeked redheaded darling, Peter, the year before.

I felt so strongly for Peter, and lacking the words to explain it all, I offered him my body. We were in my room alone, and things got pretty heated. When he backed off quickly, and said we should stop, I was too humiliated to face him again. I broke up with him, and broke both our hearts. I could not bear to do that again, not to Andrew.

He asked me out on one other occasion before he gave up on me. We remained friends and always ended up in courses together as lab partners or teammates. By senior year, I was sure that he was the right one for me. I was absolutely in love with him. I told him so, in a letter. His response was that I lost my chance.

The glitch, the first one, anyway, was that I was engaged to someone else. There was always someone else, and it had always been that way.

Neil never had much interest in spending time with me. He was a boy, after all. Our brief relationship ended in ugly manipulative maneuvers. He told me that he would never date a fat chick, oh, and I should probably watch my weight. I weighed 118 pounds at the time, but when it was over, I weighed closer 105, having completely ceased eating. I broke up with him, but he begged me to take him back, only to break up with me in front of an audience of his friends. I hated him well after high school graduation for that emotional harm. When we were in our twenties, he apologized, stating that he never knew he'd hurt me. Ah, sweet vindication, sort of.

After Neil, there was Richard. Richard wooed me in Physics class by painting my fingernails and kissing the back of my hand before we were ever introduced. He was very suave—a senior—with dark, passionate eyes. We went to a dance together, and he gave me red roses. He seemed to be always around me, which was a change from Neil's indifference. After a month, Richard started to behave strangely, playing trust games, like dangling me off-balance over his balcony railing. He scared me.

I finally broke down and had sex with Richard in the freezing back seat of his car—parked in a church parking lot, no less. It was not spectacular, which made the pregnancy scare the following month seem more bitter than sweet. One of the Civil Air Patrol advisors—I had joined, after all—gave me a pregnancy test they bought at a drug store for me to take home. It was negative.

When I told Richard, he just dismissed it with the cliché assumption that it probably wasn't his, anyway. I was outraged, silently. The next day, he missed our standing lunch date, and I found him with another girl. I was so hurt, and even more baffled by his behavior. I spent the hour being comforted by our mutual friend, Aaron.

Richard hunted me down after I left college to apologize to me for what he'd done. Apparently, our friend Aaron told Richard that he had first-hand knowledge of my promiscuity. No wonder he'd been so eager to comfort me. Kindness in the left hand and malice in the right—this was a common theme for me.

I was so angry after Richard that I wanted to behave as badly as possible. Enter Matthew, an obese, crass, acne-riddled senior who cared only about cars and sex. We made full use of each other's interests for the remainder of the school year. I hated him, as a person. He constantly reminded me that I was not as pretty or as good as the girl who dumped him before we met. I should have crushed him, but I let him hurt me until we couldn't handle any more.

The last week of the year, I actually attended my courses because Matthew had to attend his so he could graduate. That's when I met Chris: the quiet boy whose locker was across the hall. Chris was the reason that I didn't mind so much when Matthew got Mark to tell me that he was spending the summer in California, just so I would not call him.

Chris came into my life and gave me what I thought I always wanted from a boy: complete adoration. He wasn't very smart, but he was attractive. He was emotionally withdrawn, but he adored me. He carried the devotion for both of us.

Being with Chris gave me a sense of security that brought the opposite sex out into the open. For my eleventh grade year, I had no problem deflecting the occasional flirtation, because Chris was always there. By my birthday that year, I had a diamond ring on my finger. I belonged to someone.

I wanted more, but was afraid I would never find it. I was more compatible with people who could think and reason. Chris worked hard, and was very responsible. He talked about honor and duty as though they were a given in any discussion. He fathered me, in a sense, while my own father was drinking more and more, all of the time.

I tried to break up with Chris right before my high school graduation. Andrew's rejection made me want my freedom more than ever. I had a scholarship, and I was going to college in October. I had so many chances to meet someone more like me, and I wanted to be free to take them. I didn't want to be fathered any longer.

My resolve was destroyed when Chris arrived at my commencement ceremony with a giant pink box containing a dozen long-stemmed red roses. He was crying, and looked so defeated. He had purchased the roses in advance, and had no choice but to give them to me. I couldn't bear to see him hurt. More accurately, I had no idea who I was without him to tell me, so I gave in. We spent the days before he left for his summer Army Reserve duty in happy contact over the phone.

That summer, the infidelities began.

People cheat for different reasons, and I was no exception. There were different sorts of reasons for the affairs, and different results. The first time I cheated on Chris, I did it out of contempt and pride.

About two days before his return from summer encampment, I was enjoying a day off from my job at the grocery store, sunbathing in my parents' driveway. I liked lying out there, because the men in the neighborhood liked it, and Faith hated it. It was a real boost to the self-esteem, and it was much better than lying out in the back with that rotten cocker spaniel running around.

My sun worship was disturbed by calls from that particular blond-haired neighbor boy on the corner. I walked over to his fence and stood with a critical look on my face while he extolled the virtues of his newly gained sexual prowess. He had been married, he told me, and he learned a few tricks. He was not fourteen, anymore.

I reminded him that I was not twelve, and I knew better—plenty better. He continued to swear up and down that he would give me everything he never did before. I took him up on his dare.

Thirty-five seconds later, I walked down the stairs from his room and found our neighbor, Curt, sitting on the couch; I knew I had been duped.

"Been here long, Curt?" I acted as disgusted and bored as I could, "Oh, wait. You couldn't have been here more than a minute; I would have seen you when I came in."

I didn't bother to look back when Curt started laughing and taunting the liar in his own house.

When Chris came back, I did not mention the encounter. I really didn't think it was worth it. Chris and I were naturally happy to see one another again, and spent as much private, intimate time as we could for two people who still lived with their parents. It was a good summer for us, reunited joyfully, with renewed commitment. We were both looking forward to my first year of college. Soon, we would find a place to live together and begin our lives, as we should.

I can't remember what the first symptom was that got my attention, but I think Chris pointed it out before I had even formed the word in my head. My weight had not changed much, but my face had broken out with acne. My breasts were slightly puffy and sore. We drove to Ogden and got a free test from a lady at a pro-life center to confirm it: I was pregnant.

As I slumped against the wall on the floor of the old house that had been converted to the Pro-Life Center, I stared at the pile of donated baby clothes and started to cry. I knew that my life was about to end, and not just at my hand this time. I was terrified of my parents.

Chris and I drove back to Layton, and I started thinking of ways to keep my scholarship. I could complete the first quarter or two of school easily, even if I was pregnant. I reasoned that pregnancy was not a disability that could keep me from attending class. I knew girls in high school who did it, so why not college? Chris agreed that I would be able to finish around a year of school, depending on how long I had been pregnant; it could not have been very long, since he had only been in town for a few weeks.

I remembered what Richard had said, and felt sick. Chris never even doubted that the baby was his.

I was talking to Chris on the phone about how we would break the news to our parents when I caught Keri eavesdropping outside my door. The decision was made for us, as Keri betrayed me to her mother as soon as she could. I warned Chris, in case my father might want to kill him.

Faith was working at the Obstetrics clinic at the University of Utah Hospital at the time, and had a complete repertoire of clinical information prepared by the time she and my father converged on our house that night.

My parents were angry, but contained it. They said that they understood that they would not be able to help me if they scared me off by getting mad at me. Since Chris and I were planning to get married, they accepted that we were having sex. Then, they brought out the medical weaponry.

I had been taking lithium as prescribed without interruption. As a result, my father said, my baby would be so deformed that its brain would be growing on the outside of its head and had no hope of living normally. He continued, outlining some of the more serious threats to my health that would come with any pregnancy: complications due to the hypertension that I had been treated for in the past, vascular and lung damage, kidney problems, and so on. He told me that, if I ever did want a baby, I would have to go through a year of preparation, and I would not likely be able to deliver the child full term.

"So," my dad concluded, "You will be getting the pregnancy terminated."

I accepted this, in light of the horrible consequences of going ahead. Chris and I assured each other by sacrificing this one child we could have more healthy children in the future. I contacted the only reputable women's clinic in Utah that performed abortions, and made an appointment for a few days away. Chris, my father, Faith, and I would all make the drive to Salt Lake City for the appointment. Chris was going to pay the $180 fee with his credit card.

When I was a senior in high school, I remember the slander and condemnation of a couple of girls who were rumored to have had abortions, all passed in whispers when they came into the room. I was so pro-life because it made me feel safe to be that way—similar to the feeling of security that one feels when they donate to cancer research: charity or beliefs as a talisman against the cause. I took solace in the notion that they seemed to come back to school, unscathed.

My family had to wait in the outer room while I was counseled on the procedure and given the options required by state laws. I had no options, really, because I believed that I would die if I tried to keep the baby. I listened to the woman talk about the nuances of the adoption process with detachment. When she was done, I signed the form agreeing to proceed.

She then presented a number of permanent birth control options for me to consider. According to state law, I could not leave the clinic until I committed to a long-term form of passive birth control. This meant that it had to be something that worked whether I wanted it to, or not. Faith already covered this option for me, and wrangled a free implant that would last me five years. One of the doctors in her office would insert it in my arm, as soon as my cycle returned to normal. The implant met with the approval of the nurse, and I was taken back to another waiting room for the procedure.

All of the rooms in the clinic were separated with doors that sealed magnetically, like the doors in the mental hospital. A person had to be "buzzed through" by someone on the other side in order to pass from room to room.

Shortly after I was left in a room at the end of the hall, a large Middle Eastern woman who seemed like a giant to me summoned me. She spoke in clipped English, and sounded both angry and unintelligible, at once. I tried not to be afraid of her.

She told me to get on the table, with my feet in the stirrups.

"Wear only this," she said, pointing with her pen to a white gown with tiny sea-foam green diamonds all over it. "Only this, opening in the back."

She left the room and I complied as quickly as I could. The room was cold, as were the stirrups.

I closed my eyes and recalled the nurse's description of the procedure: a dilation and curettage, or D and C. The nurse promised me some Valium in an IV, and little pain.

When the big doctor returned, a pair of nurses flanked her. They looked like the little stacking Russian dolls, having popped out of her somehow. They busied themselves in preparing me for the doctor by adjusting my posture and draping me with paper sheets.

The doctor said something that I couldn't understand about my blood pressure and my medication. What I could make out accelerated my heart rate: no Valium for me. I was getting nitrous oxide. Nitrous. Even the dentist gives shots of Novocain with the nitrous oxide.

I didn't complain because I believed that I didn't have the right to complain. I deserved whatever punishment Doctor Goliath could dish out, and I deserved to take it quietly. I thought that little of myself for what I was doing.

When the procedure began, there was a mechanical noise, and the sudden sensation that my entire abdomen was being torn out by rabid tigers with dirty claws. It was the worst physical pain I had ever experienced. To this day, I have never experienced its equal. I inhaled sharply, and tried to take deep, deep inhalations of the nitrous oxide. I didn't cry out—I always think that the pain I feel is minor compared to others who have handled it better than I do. I just tried to breathe as the minutes passed.

I was crying involuntarily from the pain, which began to dull into what I imagined was the cramping ache emanating from the gaping hole left behind, though it had moved somewhat lower. I became aware that the nurses were alarmed about something.

I was hyperventilating, and my neck and chest were covered in splotchy red hives. Doctor Goliath said something about allergy to nitrous and hurried the nurses into removing the small rubber mask that was feeding me the only relief I had. She ordered one of them to get me a shot of antihistamine. I could barely hear her, over the screaming pain in my uterus. I wanted to curl into a ball, but I couldn't move until she was done with me.

The nurses left and the doctor handed me a sanitary napkin. She told me to use it, put on my clothes, and go through that door—pointing behind me—and to the right. That was the recovery room, she said, and they'd give me some painkillers. I said okay.

Then, I disobeyed her because I had no choice. After she left the room, I sat up and tried to stand, but the pain knocked me back down. I was nauseated, and I was bleeding quite a bit. I lay curled on the table, waiting for the pain to subside. A nurse came in while I was in this posture. I told her I hurt, and I couldn't get up.

The doctor came in and seemed even more annoyed—which was virtually unimaginable—and prompted me to put my feet back in the stirrups by patting my knee, and cradling the back of my ankle with her massive hand.

I complied, in a stupor. Suddenly, she was briskly poking, pressing, and pushing against my vaginal wall and cervix with her hands. The pain rose from a smolder to a flame with every touch.

"You're fine," she judged, removing her gloves. "Get up. Let's go."

I told myself that every step I could take was one step farther away from that woman and closer to home. I used that motivation somehow to manage a hobble down the hall to a yellow vinyl recliner in the recovery area. There were five other women in similar chairs, reclining sleepily as their drugs wore off. They sipped juice and watched television with bleary eyes.

I was given a single codeine pill, which I swallowed incredulously. Moments later, I rushed to the bathroom and threw it up. I was still losing blood and my skin was hot. I returned to my chair and curled into the fetal position, with my feet pushing the air as I groaned. They gave me another codeine pill. I still hurt.

The aide came over and took my temperature and blood pressure. She was fretting over them both, and told me that my family would not be permitted to see me until I calmed down. I was just upsetting myself, she said.

The codeine started to muffle the pain, and I turned over on my back and internalized any vocalizations that erupted from the pain. I sat with my knees up, and tried to appear placid. I could hear my father's angry voice on the other side of the door: the aide must have fed him that same line about me calming down before he could come over.

"Daddy?" I pled at the small window. His voice quieted into a calmer tone. I could tell he was talking through clenched teeth. I heard him mention his career choice.

The door opened, and he pushed the aide aside and came to me. He snatched the blood pressure cuff out of her hand and told me to relax. I was shivering all over violently, and the blanket the aide gave me didn't help.

I tried to focus on stillness in my mind while the cuff hissed and wilted on my arm. Soon, my dad was shouting at the aide, showing her my pressure reading. The systolic pressure was above 200, and the diastolic was nearly as high. I was getting close to stroke territory, and he was incensed. He told me that was why I was shivering. I closed my eyes and tried to recall some of the relaxation techniques from my hospital days.

In my imagination, I was lying in tall grass under a tree, next to a quiet stream, and the center of my body was on fire.

My father finally convinced the nurses to release me into his care, and we left. I slept in the back of the van with my head on Chris's lap until we reached home.

Sadly, home was the same as ever. Chris ran to the store (literally) to buy me some juice, and Mark, Keri, and Jessica got into a screaming, wrestling match complete with Jessica's high-pitched squeals, about three feet from the couch where I was trying to sleep. No one cared.

After Chris left to go to work, my father pointed out that it was my turn to clean the kitchen and take out the trash. I was accepting a punishment that I felt I deserved, and did not complain when I began to bleed heavily again after dragging our weighted steel cans to the curb.

My wounds healed in time. The implant was inserted in my arm, and I carried on as normally as I could. My pro-life views changed considerably, but I didn't feel any emotional backlash or loss from what I'd done. I supposed that I had escaped the depression most women experience.

Chris and I were as close as ever, though his parents continued to hate me. I was not worthy of their son.

School was a great distraction for me, though it was very similar to high school. I recognized many of the other students, and Chris was always there. My Advanced Placement credits knocked out most of the fluff, and I was taking care of the remainder of the general credits with courses I enjoyed: psychology, human development, and communications.

Near the middle of my first term, I was blind-sided by the Human Development text. When I saw the depictions of a fetus at eight weeks, I cried for two hours, solid. I told Chris about it, and he cried, too. We decided not to talk about it, again.

CHAPTER ELEVEN: THIS WAY TO THE GREAT EGRESS

As the weather got warmer, and I got more manic and hungry to feed my ego—and my ludicrous libido—the philandering began, again. I didn't have to look very far, in my workplace—a grocery store full of bagboys, stock boys, and managers—to find a willing participant. I never considered my own reputation. Consequences are for those who have the time to think about their actions, as you may recall.

When I finally moved out of my parents' house and into an apartment with Chris, I was sure that my indiscretions would end. College made that somewhat more difficult, with all types of men that wanted to marry me, sleep with me, or be my sugar daddy. I was still learning how to say "no," in those days.

Chris and I shared a studio apartment for the first year, and then moved to a duplex. A coworker of Chris's and a friend of ours, named Pat, suggested the place—the other half belonged to his family—and it was a good deal. We had more space, and I got a built-in best friend. Pat helped me blow off steam every now and then when the stodgy, conservative Chris started to annoy me.

I always thought of Pat as the safest male friend I would ever have, because there was no risk of him ever being attracted to me, or me to him. He was pure.

With the larger place, it seemed that Chris spent more time working. He might have been trying to advance his career at McDonald's, or pay for the car we purchased after mine died. I wasn't sure why he was gone so often, but it left my hands idle. I did plenty that I should not have to keep them busy.

When a person commits a terrible crime, one often hears about the perpetrator being caught for a lesser offense: an axe murderer apprehended in routine traffic stop, or something of the sort. My minor transgression was a fat 15-year old boy in the neighborhood who was infatuated with me. I wasn't having sex with him, or doing anything naked in his vicinity. I'm not sure what Chris heard, but he was plenty angry. He poured on the guilt relentlessly, talking about how I betrayed him and he'd done nothing to deserve it. In shame and anger, I left—though not far, I was sleeping in Pat's room, on the couch, next door. I went over to our side of the duplex when I knew Chris was gone.

In the manic mind, this was completely sensible.

After a few days with Pat as my only testosterone-based influence, he started looking appealing to me. He was charming and attractive, despite his oddball boyishness. I had to get out and talk to Chris before I ruined my safe friendship by saying something stupid. I waited in our living room for him to come home, and the fighting commenced.

We argued about every little disagreement that we had for a year. Every difference of opinion and every slight was fair game. I cried and yelled, but the main theme of the whole debacle was that I was awful, and he was perfect. I hurt him, and I needed to beg for his forgiveness—that was Chris's position. I didn't like being humbled, or blamed. I had grievances too: he ignored me, he hated my friends, and he was terrible in bed. I threw the last one in to keep him busy—a little Schiller family cruelty.

However, that one backfired on me. When I started to berate his sexual performance as a last attempt to get the upper hand in the argument, he turned the tables on me.

"Yeah? Well, that's not what Kristy said!" As soon as he said it, we both ceased to make any noise. I wasn't even sure I was still breathing.

"Come again? I don't think I just heard you," I could feel my reason dissolve in the rage that was boiling from the bottom of my being, upward. I started to shake.

He repeated it, coolly. He had an affair, himself. One of the girls at work was interested in him, and she invited him to her house. He went, because it made him feel good about himself. Sure, she was married, and had children, but it didn't matter to him. She wanted him.

His reasons sounded familiar to me, and I should have identified with his humanity. I didn't— the anger I felt was consuming any compassion or understanding I might have had for him. Mania turns ugly when the fun wears out—it becomes malice and paranoia. I was seething as my mind turned the scenario over, remembering the tacky, frizzy blonde Kristy in her McDonald's uniform.

He told me that it happened one time—only one time—and he told her that it wouldn't happen again, despite her requests for a repeat performance. I found this less believable, but the result was the same. Her husband had gone looking for Chris. In order to avoid the near-fatal beating he deserved, he had called me with some fabricated ruse, and I dropped everything to drive to the mall and pick him up. I remembered the day well. He had appealed to my sympathy with his concocted emergency.

My sick and tortured soul fed on itself, and fed on pain. I knew I wouldn't be happy until the bandage was ripped fully away.

"Tell me what happened. What did you do?" I still don't know why I asked. I consider it a push from fate. "Did you fuck a married woman with kids there?"

He must have mistaken my restraint for detachment, because he answered me in a matter-of-fact tone.

"She sat me on her couch, and she kissed me passionately," he was not making any eye contact with me, or he would have seen that I was already crying. He exhaled in a long sigh, and said, "Then she gave me a really good blowjob."

The snap I felt inside myself at that moment had to be the lock on a deep door that held the most primal darkness at bay. A guttural noise began to poor out of my throat, and I became blind to all but my goal. I raced down the hall, though I couldn't feel my legs moving. I rounded the corner in the bedroom, and found my quarry on a small decorator table in the corner: the 9 mm semi-automatic handgun. In one swift motion, I had lifted the heavy gun from the table, turned off the safety with a flip of my thumb, and cocked it back with my free hand.

Before I could decide what I wanted to do with the power in my hand, Chris appeared in the doorway. My pain told me that I should make him watch me blow my skull apart. My fury told me that he should go first. In the interim, I held the gun at my chest level, and pointed it toward the ceiling, waving it as I spoke.

"I don't want to live another day, knowing what you did to me, Chris." I was crying. Sanity had left the neighborhood. "It's not just that you cheated—and with a scummy, white-trash married WHORE from McDonald's—but you made me feel like shit for even considering it, myself."

I began to weaken, physically. I wanted to sit, to lie, and to sleep.

"Ronnie, I know. I'm sorry; it was a horrible thing to do. I feel awful, and I shouldn't have hurt you," he didn't come near me, but lifted his hand in a subtle motion. "Please, Ronnie, hand me the gun."

I didn't lift my head as I brought my hands together and released the clip from the butt of the gun. I handed both parts to Chris, and dropped to my knees without a sound. He removed one round from the chamber, and then popped out a second.

"I guess it's a good thing I kept a round chambered in the gun. You double-loaded it when you cocked it, so it was just jammed."

We started to talk, and apologized to each other. By the time the sun had set, we were having make-up sex in the living room. In a moment of post-coital bliss (or, stupidity), Chris suggested that we marry. I agreed.

The date was set for mid-May.

Chris's parents were the sorts who thrived on material displays of wealth. His stepmother was pushy and opinionated, and felt it her duty to overrun the entire wedding process. My every choice was deemed incorrect, so the planning was a constant struggle. Things were coming along nicely, despite the short notice, when we hit our worst obstacle.

We had selected the Air Force Base Chapel for the ceremony, and a log cabin nearby for the reception site. We had a caterer, a florist, and decorations at the ready. I had a store-bought dress, and my best friend made a veil for me. I was in the process of getting dresses made for Keri and Jessica—those ladies were shaped like the stepsisters in Cinderella, with one tall and too thin, and the other short and wide.

Chris and I had dinner with my parents to arrange the tuxedo rentals. I knew they had little money to spare, so I asked them only to cover the cost of their own clothing. My father needed a tuxedo, and Faith needed a dress with colors similar to the ones I chose for the bridal party.

"What about Mark?" Faith added, "He's the best man, right? Doesn't he need a tux?"

Chris explained that his full brother had just moved in with his parents after living in Canada with his mother, and that he—not Mark, or one of Chris's stepbrothers—was chosen to be the best man.

The argument that erupted from that spawned a fight that ended with my entire family boycotting the wedding. My father began to leave harassing drunken messages on my answering machine all night long, threatening Chris and me. I wouldn't take up Faith's defense; I still remembered Mark's role in my rape. I wouldn't argue to save his life, much less, secure his place in my wedding.

The wedding was beautiful and without error, though less than ten seats in the chapel were occupied.

Three months later, in early August, Chris took an opportunity to join the Army full time. I was happy about the notion that he would finally quit working at McDonald's, after four years of that embarrassment. I didn't think about what he would have to do when he joined—leave me for six months, to train.

I was supposed to share a nice apartment, on the government dollar, with Pat. Pat was supposed to keep an eye on me for Chris. That worked for about one month.

When the mania set in, I stopped sleeping and started smoking and drinking. My work hours were strange: 4:00 AM to 11:00 AM. I partied and drank all night, sometimes napping in the afternoon. In early October, Pat paid up his portion of the lease, and moved out in the middle of the night.

I partied and shopped to fill the time. To fill the space, I led a parade of boys and men and young kids in and about my house. The kids came to get beer that they couldn't buy on their own. The boys and men came for whatever they could get from me. I was out of control.

I bought a treadmill and started running for a half hour every night. I stopped eating, except for the occasional bowl of rice. I dropped thirty pounds before Christmas.

I was impulsive and lean, and braless as usual, when I wandered over to a convenience store at 2:30 am to buy a quart of beer to keep me entertained while I washed my clothes in the 24-hour Laundromat. The guy behind the counter smiled obviously, and watched me intently as I made my selection so that he failed to notice that my teen companions were stealing all the merchandise they could grab. He had that special quality that I liked: he liked me.

In this surreal time, I experienced one of the most wonderful gifts of fate. Willie, prompted by qualities of mine in his daughter, tracked me down and called me on the phone. I had a chance to catch up on his life, and hear about his family. He had missed me, much as I had missed him. He told me that mother's attorney had arranged for Clifton's release after two months served. They stayed together for a long time, but weren't together any longer. Willie and Annie Jean moved out before the trial. Annie Jean was recently diagnosed with schizophrenia, like their father.

Mother had forbidden anyone to speak my name in her presence.

I told Willie that I was thinking about leaving Chris, and he suggested that I move to Florida and live with him in near the beautiful beach. I told him I would consider it, though I was afraid to be near my mother.

I ran into the smiley counter guy a few more times, as I visited the store to buy beer or cigarettes for my minor friends over the next month. I was able to recognize his little car in the parking lot. In the end of March, I returned from a night at the movies with a dear friend—whom I wanted to date—and his father—who wanted to date me. I was all primed from the evening of attention, and decided to make my move, buying a pack of unneeded cigarettes for no apparent reason, other than to meet the clerk.

We talked all night, and went back to my place for coffee—but instead had sex on my living room floor, instead. Shortly after that, Jason the Clerk sat on my couch and cheered me on as I called Chris and told him I wanted a divorce. He moved into the apartment within a week of that event. When a person is moving so fast mentally, such rapid-succession events seem normal, and there are no consequences to consider, or so it seemed.

Willie didn't like the sound of Jason. He thought the relationship would come and go, and urged me to think about living in Florida. Much the way that I married Chris to disprove the theory that all high school sweethearts divorced (and failed), I took Willie's statement as a challenge. I was determined to make my relationship with Jason work.

I didn't speak to my brother and best childhood friend, Willie, for ten years.

CHAPTER TWELVE: SAFETY

I enjoyed the waiting room in Dr. Santo's office not for the art, which was bland and only briefly engaging, but for the magazines. I didn't subscribe to magazines because I found them a waste of paper and space: they usually became unread piles of clutter in my home. Santo's lobby was stocked with some great reads for a variety of tastes. Aside from the usual sports magazines, gossip rags, celebrity watchers, and fashion fare, there were a few choice publications for a more specialized group of readers. My favorites were the Johns Hopkins Magazine and the quarterly from the Nature Conservancy. I didn't mind a long wait in this office—unlike the gynecologist's office, which was choked with floral patterns and stocked with women's magazines like "Ladies' Home Journal." That was a vile place.

My visits with Dr. Santo had grown unproductive in the last month or two. I had not scheduled any new appointments to follow, and he was preparing to move to a new practice, so he did not set them up for me. I viewed this as an opportunity to break away cleanly.

Dr. Santo helped me tremendously in the year that we'd been meeting—I even referred a friend or two that I thought could use his help through a tough time. I never met such an honest man, so straightforward and without judgment. We had developed a friendship, so much that he offered to visit me in the hospital when I thought surgery was in my future. Just to see me; he was like that.

He had done a superb job of setting me on the path to understanding what drives my decisions, and where my weaknesses were misleading me. Ultimately, I had to use the knowledge he helped me discover to make the best choices for myself. I had to walk the path that gave me the most stable sort of happiness.

The nurse practitioner and I found the medication regimen that kept me from falling prey to the big, seasonal cycles that had disrupted my life for nearly twenty years. While nothing seems to be a permanent fix in a system as dynamic as the human body, I felt hopeful, knowing that I was armed with the perception to know when the chemistry was out of balance. My first year of continuous sanity had been productive, positive, and rich with introspection. I found it far easier to consider the questions as to why I made mistakes when I was able to take the time to consider that I had made them.

A year of living without Jason proved to be beneficial. There were times that were difficult for me to handle, and I felt overwhelmed. I felt defeated, and wished for someone to make the decisions for me. I discovered, in time, that a person is much stronger when they accept that they have to rely upon their own abilities to deal with stress, or to solve a problem. It is a "training-wheel effect": I relied upon other people to make decisions for me, for better or worse, simply because I could. When I could no longer accept their judgment or rely on their support, I found that I could do a much better job on my own. Dr. Santo helped me to remove the training wheels, but the strength and ability were mine.

I was proud of my accomplishments and of how much I had grown. I didn't harbor too much anger—reasonably, there was some sense of betrayal—over the discovery that Jason had been lying about the cancer. He had also lied about Floyd being angry with me. These truths were revealed in a devastating tandem, when Floyd finally tracked down my phone number. It would have been easy to feed a vengeful urge against Jason, but the self-destruction was counter to the person I had become. I wished Jason a long, long, introspective life—perhaps with a touch of cancer, at the end.

I glanced at the clock, and hoped that Dr. Santo would be a little bit late, so I could finish reading the article about racism in the modern republican South. I always found the culture of rural separatists to be fascinating and disturbing.

"Ronnie." Just in time. He stood in the doorway, with his foot as a doorstop.

We spent a few minutes discussing the article I read. He asked the analytical questions that a psychologist would ask, such as, "How do you feel about that?" I told him that I thought extremism on either side of the racial issue was still wrong. For a publication to characterize the entire South as a bunch of gun-rack pickup truck Klan hicks was irresponsible and unethical in terms of journalistic integrity. He nodded, without comment. I said that it was also wrong for people to be gun-rack pickup truck Klan hicks, and unfortunate that the exaggerated ignorance of the few staggered the statistics. He nodded to this, as well. The man was no idiot—I saw a title by Henry Rollins occupying some of the limited space on his bookshelf, which I regarded with silent joy.

"Oh, well. Can't change the world," I concluded, "Just me."

"Speaking of which," he pulled out the chart, "what was your last assignment from me?"

I applauded the nicely executed segue, to which he smiled and bowed his head slightly. My last assignment was related to some of the positive changes in my life. I found those to be more of a challenge to accept than the catastrophic or predictably disappointing times. I was waiting for the other shoe to drop, to use an idiom. In my life, it seemed to be virtually raining "other shoes."

"I was supposed to accept that Ronnie deserves to be happy," I told him.

"And?"

"And, it's working out pretty well."

I explained my new approach: I just left it alone. I didn't try to steer the circumstances in the direction that I wanted. I suppressed the urge to sabotage my success so I could be right about the ever-present nature of failure. I did not question the reasons behind the kindness of others, but I did not rely upon or expect anything from others.

"How's that working for you?" His question seemed more conversational than analytical. He was taking very few notes.

It was working great, and I could think of nothing else to say on the subject. Real happiness was a strange thing, in my observation. I tried to elaborate for him, but explaining emotions to other people is sometimes like explaining the view of a ray of the sun to someone who was born blind. You lack the perspective reference point.

Actual happiness seemed to resound at a lower frequency than manic happiness. It was low and constant, without the elation and the spikes of extremity.

"Disappointing?" He asked, predictably.

"At first, it was," I was truthful. I was not sure if I liked being stable as much as I enjoyed the buzz and the nervous hum of mania.

I was falling in love—or easing in, I suppose. I didn't feel dizzying heights, or sickening longing. I didn't feel ecstatic chills, or any of the things that you hear in songs. I was not experiencing the sort of epiphany that inspires poetry and drastic life changes. I was simply happy. Not depressed, not excited: I was just happy. I wasn't sure it was right, but I wouldn't change it.

"What are you going to do, now?"

I thought for only a moment, and told him, "I don't know. I want to just leave it alone." I shrugged. Everything was going so well for me at home, and at work. I felt that I had earned some peace. That, alone, was a big step for me.

Dr. Santo expressed his approval. He was proud of me, and of what I had accomplished through hard work and thought. I had turned my life around, and had broken some habits that would have led me to painful disappointment with every effort. I deserved to be happy.

"Remember that," he advised me. It was the last advice he would give me.

Praise made me uncomfortable. It's hard to beat conditioning, and years of experience, that underlined for me the fact that I was unworthy of praise—or, the people who helped to raise me thought so. I remind myself to consider the source, always. Extremism, on either side, is a bad thing.

For the first time in thirty years of extreme highs and lows, I had found a sunny patch of middle ground. Though not perfect, I was secure in the feeling that I possessed the potential to live—not just survive. That was what I had always wanted.

As I drove home, I pondered a long list in my head of things that brought me happiness, and made life worth living.

Number One was behind the wheel, smiling back from the rear view mirror.

Epilogue

It has been almost a decade since I wrote this. It's hard for me to read. The emotional undercurrent is strong enough to pull me under, even after all of the time I have had to heal. It's hard to believe that I was that weak, codependent person.

Is my life perfect today? Certainly not. It is my life, and I control the direction more adeptly than I ever have. A perfect life is either a life full of denial or devoid of risk. Neither of those options appeals to me.

Since I wrote this, I have seen my father die, my stepmother turn against me, lost another marriage to alcoholism and domestic violence, and was diagnosed with cervical cancer. I have also earned a Master of Science degree, survived cancer, bought my first house, brought home my first dog, and married a man whom I took ten years to get to know before we even kissed. This is my longest-lasting marriage yet, and it will be my last. My life is about balance, and working to tip the scales toward the positive side or holding it all up until I can.

Thanks to this book, my little brother, "Brandon" found me. He is an amazing adult, and I could not be happier that he contacted me. His mother turned out much as I thought she might, but not as bad as she was. At least I know it wasn't personal.

I have seen complaints about my story being a long brag about my sexual conquests. That saddens me, as it was not the intent. My relationships are a symptom of the sexual abuse, verbal abuse, alienation, and abandonment I experienced as a child. There is nothing proud or boastful about the stories that I relate here. They are simply part of the dysfunction that held me back until I recognized the truth.

The concept of calling the devil by its name is crucial to self-observation and self-awareness. By confessing all that I have, I know my truth. It makes me stronger. That awareness is what I want for the people who read this.

Thank you for reading my story.

Made in the USA
San Bernardino, CA
09 April 2014